THE NATIVES WERE FRIENDLY
SO WE STAYED THE NIGHT

Noel Barber first became well known as
foreign correspondent of the *Daily Mail*. He
was the first Briton to reach the South Pole
after Scott, was stabbed five times covering the
wars in Morocco, and was shot in the head
during the Hungarian uprising. A serious car
crash ended his career as a correspondent but
enabled him to become a full-time writer. He
was the author of several works of non-fiction
and in his seventies, became a bestselling
novelist. He lived in London with his wife
Titina. Noel Barber died in 1988.

By the same author

Fiction
Tanamera
A Farewell to France
A Woman of Cairo
The Other Side of Paradise
The Weeping and the Laughter

History
The Week France Fell
Seven Days of Freedom
Lords of the Golden Horn
The War of the Running Dogs
Sinister Twilight
From the Land of Lost Content
The Black Hole of Calcutta
The Singapore Story
The Fall of Shanghai

Autobiography
The Natives Were Friendly
Fires of Spring
Strangers in the Sun
Life with Titina

Travel
The White Desert
Trans-Siberian
Distant Places

Politics
How Strong Is America?
The Menace of Japan

War
A Handful of Ashes
Prisoner of War
The Flight of the Dalai Lama

General
Conversations with Painters
Newspaper Reporting

Juvenile
Adventures at Both Poles
Let's Visit the USA

In Partnership
Cities (with Rupert Croft-Cooke)
Hitler's Last Hope (with Ernest Phillips)
An Island to Oneself (with Tom Neale)

TANAMERA, A FAREWELL TO FRANCE, A WOMAN OF CAIRO, THE OTHER SIDE OF PARADISE, and THE WEEPING AND THE LAUGHTER are all available from Coronet.

The Natives Were Friendly . . .
So We Stayed the Night

Noel Barber

CORONET BOOKS
Hodder and Stoughton

First published in Great Britain
in 1977 by Macmillan London
Ltd.

First published in paperback by
Robin Clark Ltd. in 1979

Coronet edition 1985
Second impression 1989

British Library C.I.P.

Barber, Noel
    The natives were friendly – so
we stayed the night. –
(Rev. ed.)
1. Barber, Noel   2. Journalists
– England –
Biography
I. Title
070'.92'4   PN5123.B29

ISBN 0-340-38081-0

Photoset by Rowland
Phototypesetting Ltd., Bury St.
Edmunds, Suffolk. Printed and
bound in Great Britain for Hodder
and Stoughton Paperbacks, a
division of Hodder and Stoughton
Ltd., Mill Road, Dunton Green,
Sevenoaks, Kent TN13 2YA
(Editorial Office: 47 Bedford
Square, London WC1B 3DP) by
Richard Clay Ltd., Bungay,
Suffolk.

CONTENTS

FOR TITINA,
WITH LOVE

Foreword to revised edition

AT THE AGE of four I was taken prisoner by the Germans. At the age of seventy I became a novelist. A great deal happened in the years between, ranging from three months I spent in the South Seas to three months in Antarctica, from two years in Singapore to two years in San Francisco. But always I have wanted to write, ever since at the age of nine I produced my first book (all of thirty pages) and charged Mama's friends one old penny each to read it. I have been writing ever since.

Like a dream miraculously come true I have been writing and travelling, for a living, all my life, and I have loved every moment of it, from Acapulco to Zanzibar.

This book is mainly about the second part of my life, for even in middle age life has always started afresh for me when I seemed to have reached the end of a certain road. At thirty-six I became an editor in Paris. At forty-three I became a foreign correspondent, but only because my editorial chair collapsed. At fifty-three I started writing my 'reconstruction' books only because a car crash landed me in hospital for six months. In my late fifties, when I thought myself tied to a desk, a new life opened up when I became a full-time author. And finally I realised what had always been my *real* boyhood dream when, at the age of seventy, I published my first novel. Even better – a bestselling novel!

Inevitably some famous names spatter these pages, but please do not imagine they are deliberately dropped to add spice. A world of hoity-toity difference separates the name-dropper from the name-user. If I write casually that I once dined with the Sultan of Johore (as I did), omitting to mention that I had never previously met the gentleman and was one of a dozen guests, that is name-dropping. But if I add that after the coffee the Sultan (as he did) offered me two pretty girls and the use of a bed, that is name-using.

My work has brought me in contact with the rich and famous, but this is still a book about a boy who set out to see the world, not to try and conquer it – heaven forbid – but to enjoy it, to savour it, to work in it, to be a part of it. And to write about it.

Enjoying one's work, being stimulated by it, requires energy and good health. Touch wood, I have both. Born in 1909, I have nearly died seven times, but always from accidents. Though I have had sixty-seven stitches in my head, I have never had a headache. Though I was stabbed by an Arab in Casablanca (in the back, of course), I can still touch my toes. Though my left thigh was broken in five places, I still walk briskly at seventy-five. Though I drink three triple Scotches before dinner each evening – plus whatever is to follow – I have never had a hangover. Around midnight I might begin to feel my years, but by God, with each new dawn, I am never a day over twenty-one.

N.B.

London, 1975–7, and 1985

1

APRIL IN PARIS

THIS BOOK IS not about tennis, but . . .

It was like a dream. On an immaculate red centre court, I was representing Britain in an international tennis match at Monte Carlo. The sun danced on the shimmering Mediterranean, the bougainvillaea blazed on the stands, as six stalwart Britons of the International Club prepared to engage the flower of Monégasque manhood: Britons with legendary Wimbledon names like Pat Hughes and Nigel Sharpe, and Vladimir Landau, Monaco's Davis Cup player.

Of course I had no right to be there. The rules of the International Club clearly stipulate that to become a member a player must have carried his racquet overseas for club or country. Well, one member had mislaid his club, country, racquet or self; I happened to be staying in Monte Carlo with my boss, Lord Rothermere, who was a member of the I.C. Rather than ruin the game, rules were bent, shorts pressed, shirts donned, socks stretched, racquets twanged, balls bounced, and here I was.

My partner was slim, six feet four, and looked uncannily like Gary Cooper. He was also a hell of a good player. Vladimir Landau of Monaco, one of our opponents, who knew every grain of red sand on those slow, slow courts, opened with his filthy sliced service. It dropped in front of my racquet, leered at me, turned sharp right, and I never saw it again.

We lost the first set, scraped through to win the second. The decider went to six-all, then our opponents dropped their serve after one match point, and finally at 40–30 my partner sent an ace whizzing past my ear and we had won.

11

Now it is clearly impossible, after sweating for nearly two hours, and snatching victory, to turn round and say breathlessly, 'Good shot, milord!' From the heart I cried, 'Esmond, you played a bloody marvellous game.' It was the start of a beautiful friendship.

No more about tennis. But in a way this match in the mid-forties was characteristic of a new life that opened up to me after the end of the European war. Not that life had been dull before that. I had already lived and worked in Mexico, Singapore, Copenhagen, San Francisco, not to mention England. I had travelled half-way round the world on a tramp steamer, across Siberia in a train, aloft with the RAF. I had a beautiful Danish mother, whose unphonetic maiden name of Lysberg (pronounced *Lewsbare*) was protected by royal decree so that no other family could use it (if they wanted to or could spell it, that is). My hard-working father was managing director of a thriving business in Yorkshire. I had two brothers. We were a closely-knit family. On the debit side I had written nineteen books and thrown each one away.

But all that was a different world, no better, no worse, than the world that faced me when, shortly before VE day, at the ripe old age of thirty-five, I arrived in Paris as editor of the *Continental Daily Mail* – a post I held for eight years before becoming a foreign correspondent and finally, still later, realising my first dream of writing books to earn my living.

The new life brought me into contact with the famous and infamous. Darling Mama was not only young and beautiful – married at sixteen, naughty girl; she had taught me how to use a knife and fork so I was frequently invited a second time, and over the years many acquaintances became good friends.

One's early life is never forgotten; the past plays its part in the present. How can one fall in love without remembering the first time? How can one describe the delight of seeing one's book in a shop window without recalling the years of agonising failure? I was talking to

Picasso in his shop-cum-workroom at Vallauris when a
woman bridled at the price he demanded for a flimsy
sketch. 'Madame,' he replied stonily, 'that sketch took me
half an hour – and fifty years – to draw.'

Past, present, future, all are indivisible, for as Eliot
wrote, 'In my end is my beginning.'

After we had showered and downed a very dry martini
that day in Monte Carlo, Esmond Rothermere and I repaired to the Casino, and the first person to whom he
introduced me was Sidney Beer, the orchestral conductor.
In those days – not so long ago – the Salles Privées had all
the charm of carefully preserved faded elegance. The lofty
rooms, the dinner jackets, the flunkeys in their knee-
breeches, reeked of *La Belle Époque*, and one had the
feeling that hidden store-rooms were crammed with old
velvet to be used each time the salons were refurbished.
We used the place as a club, and the thought of gambling
never entered my head until I discovered that Sidney Beer
was that rare individual, a man who had once actually
broken the bank at Monte Carlo. Was it an omen? I was
flushed with success (and a second martini); moreover, it
was my birthday. I had been born on the ninth day of the
ninth month of 1909, so there was only one number on
which to bet. Not wishing to display undue rashness before
my boss, I sauntered off with some casual excuse and
changed everything I had in my pocket – the equivalent of
about £70 – into chips. I put £10 on number nine on each
of the three roulette tables, another £10 on each 5–9 *carré*.
I put it all on at once so that no one would have time to
discover what I had been doing after I lost.

The three wheels spun round almost simultaneously.
Slightly stupefied I watched the first ball click into number
nine. Then the second. Then the third.

With the sang-froid of the seasoned gambler, I sauntered
from table to table gathering up my winnings of around
£1500, tossing the odd plaque here and there to grateful
croupiers. A glass of Moet et Chandon, a Romeo and
Juliet, helped to reinforce my decision that, for me, this

was the night of the big game. Nine was obviously my lucky number, and since nine was also the perfect number to draw at chemmy, I walked over to the table, looking for a vacant chair.

At that moment a hand touched my shoulder and all of Esmond's six feet four inches looked down on me. It is hard to describe his very special way of speaking, in which he accents words strongly, often lifting his voice a semitone at the same time, as when he says, 'Well, *really*!' or 'I *must* say.'

'Well, I *must* say,' he said now, 'that was quite a *coup*. I saw it *all*. It really *was*. But I do think you'd better be sensible. *Much* better, I assure you, if I take the money now.'

Before I could say *'Banco'* he seized all my chips, and handed back a hundred pounds' worth with the remark, 'I'll give you the rest the day you leave. Then you'll be one of the few men who ever made a profit out of the Casino.'

I lost the £100 in a few minutes. But I did leave Monte Carlo nearly £1500 richer than when I arrived.

I needed the money, for though the position of Editor had a resounding ring to it, there was no corresponding clink in my pocket. There were many reasons for this. My salary had to be modest, for though thousands avidly bought the *Daily Mail*, nobody wanted to advertise in it. The war still raged in the Pacific. Rationing, bomb damage, currency restrictions, travel embargoes precluded the prospect of tourism. There was no reason why anyone should advertise in an English-language newspaper published abroad.

Because the paper was bought by thousands of British troops in Europe, the Bank of England granted permission for our parent company to export the money needed to run a car, pay the driver, and rent my apartment. But when it came to adjusting salaries, the old lady of Threadneedle Street became mean; that kind of money had to come out of the Paris till. And with a staff numbering nearly two hundred – for we printed the paper on our own presses in the rue du Sentier – there was nothing to spare.

Though my salary was small, I did have some perks. Since transport in Paris was chaotic, I was provided with a car and driver called Roger. The car was not only for my personal use but to transport the staff, and for the use of any executives who visited Paris, but basically it was mine.

I also had a furnished apartment in the rue des Saints-Pères on the Left Bank; it was extremely elegant, situated at the back of a courtyard (with a concierge peeping from her hut), up wide, winding stairs, opening on to a handsome room. I had a dining room that could seat twelve. The only item missing among the beautiful furniture was a piano, and this I was able to hire.

Since this was the only apartment I had been able to find after weeks of searching, I was delighted to be saddled with a problem which I did not think it politic to mention to London. The lady who owned the flat (and badly needed the rent) could not bear to part with her devoted man-servant, a tall, dignified Korean called Li, so his services were included in an augmented rent to ensure that when better times came and my landlady returned to her flat, Li would still be there. He was a treasure. Shuffling around in his carpet slippers, Li cooked, cleaned, washed, ironed, and refused to have any female help in the house. He did everything himself, starting each morning with a chore no one else has ever thought fit to perform for me. In a city where newspapers are not delivered, but folded and sent by post, Li each morning ironed the *Daily Mail* before brewing my coffee. And there is no better way to greet the dawn than to be awakened by the smell of a freshly pressed newspaper.

I was certainly not paid a starvation wage, but it was hard for people in Britain, where for nearly five years expenditure had been controlled by short supply, to realise that any kind of luxury – not just the sort Li represented for me – was available in the Paris black market if you had the money to pay for it. Though I personally abhorred the black market, it was a perfectly natural phenomenon to the businessmen whom I had to entertain from time to time. To many Parisians in 1945, the major problem they faced when eating in a black-market restaurant lay not in the £20–£30 a head it cost, but in finding a table in the crowded restaurant; even though in those days £20 a head for lunch seemed enormous, though by now, in the London of the eighties, lunch for two can cost £100 or more.

Then we had a stroke of good fortune, when Duff Cooper, the Ambassador, agreed that British members of the *Daily Mail* staff, many of whom were married to Frenchwomen and had been interned, should receive British Army rations. Once a week the faithful Roger deposited me at the office, then took Alex Potter, the loyal and stalwart chief reporter, to collect tins of Spam, sausages, shrimp paste, powdered eggs and, above all, duty-free drink – a real boon, as black-market Scotch cost £10 a bottle, the equivalent now of, say, £25.

Ah me! The summer of '45! It sounds like the title of a romantic film, in which I was playing the lead (though the leading ladies seemed to change from time to time). In retrospect it never seemed to rain. The candles were blowing off the chestnut trees by the time I arrived, and their pink snow was being swept away. The city was suffused with its special blue-grey haze, the boulevards were alive with pretty girls in equally pretty dresses and an apparently never-ending supply of PX stockings. I was so much in love with the tree-lined streets, the gaily decorated pavement cafés, that more often than not I walked to the office, simply to breathe the air of the most beautiful capital in the world, and share the moment when its citizens were still drunk on the heady wine of freedom – before they opened a second bottle, only to find it corked.

At this time I was married to a girl called Helen whom I had met in Singapore in 1938, but she spent a great deal of her time in London. Though we were always happy in each other's company, the strains that would lead to eventual divorce were already showing, so that as I started to live a new life in Paris I *felt* like a single man. Paris opened up wonderful, exciting avenues that I had never experienced. Walking home alone at 5 a.m. after closing a door quietly behind me, singing to myself because I was so happy, had never seemed so wonderful before.

There were of course two masks to the face of Paris; life did not revolve round Le Quarante-Cinq, the latest 'in' night club. Behind the graceful lilacs blooming in the Luxembourg gardens stood the empty pastry shops in the near-by boulevard Saint-Michel. Behind the summery dresses were the empty faces of those who had suffered. Behind the diplomatic convoys of sleek American cars trundling lorries were bringing back cargoes of half-dead – yet, miraculously, half-alive – Frenchmen from the concentration camps of Germany. And behind the rings of black marketeers, filching their butter and steaks from the peasants for the restaurants, were families who had not enough to eat.

It was a year of turmoil. Roosevelt died – and so, for that matter, did Hitler. Truman was polishing the atom bomb to be dropped in August. Churchill was out of office, de Gaulle was in – or was he? The Americans had reservations, and for two months refused to recognise de Gaulle even though he was patently running the country with the approval of the French – an American act of stupidity that made de Gaulle hate the Americans until he died, and another instance, as Duff Cooper put it (in *Old Men Forget*), 'of harm that has been done by the reluctance of men to accept readily what they know they will have to accept in the end.'

Not that de Gaulle was perfect, for 1945 was also the year of vengeance – not against the Germans, but against the French traitors paraded in staged purge trials at times worthy of Soviet Russia. Often the men involved were the victims of private grudges. Many trials were shabby mockeries of justice in this shabby post-war Europe, none more so than the vicious vendetta against the aged Marshal

Pétain: not because of Pétain, who was a vain and doddering old man, but because of the hypocrisy with which politicians who had sat comfortably on the fence in 1940 now came forward so eagerly to testify against him. De Gaulle could have stopped this and many sickening lesser trials had he not been so bigoted. Instead Europe was treated to the unsavoury spectacle of a curious blood lust on the part of the French, a kind of hysterical insistence by the lucky ones that France could only prove she had risen from the ashes by burning a few scapegoats.

2

THE BEST THINGS IN
LIFE ARE FREE

THE OFFICES OF the *Continental Daily Mail* were lodged in
a narrow five-storey building in an equally narrow street,
the rue du Sentier, off the Grands Boulevards, the upper
floors being reached by a rickety lift that held only two
people and trembled violently, as did most of the passengers after reading an ominous notice advising them to
descend on foot.

A succession of thirsty ex-soldiers in uniform guarded
the front entrance, though frequently from the zinc bar of
the bistro next door, where Marie-Lou, the owner, knew
to the nearest centime how much most members of the
staff earned, thus enabling her to gauge to a nicety their
credit ratings.

We were a very happy group, at least I like to think so,
though inevitably I was not popular with some members
of the staff who found it hard to equate my high-sounding
title with the fact that I did not have the authority to give
any member of the staff an increase of even 10 francs a
week. I did try to help by arranging for the office to
subsidise (out of that magic column 'sundry expenses') a
steak a day which Marie-Lou offered at half the price of
any other steak in Paris. Marie-Lou might not have been
Michelin-rated, and I dare say the odd bit of horse strayed
into her kitchens from time to time, but the small editorial
staff did get one square meal most evenings.

The bulk of our staff – those in the composing and
machine rooms – posed no feeding problems, for though
the French government proudly proved to the world that
it was pegging prices to stave off inflation, it did this

19

only by imposing a five-hour day, so that most of our compositors worked for two papers – ironically, the right-wing *Daily Mail* and, later in the night, the Communist *Humanité* across the road.

The *Continental Daily Mail* was of course a quirky news-paper. It attracted young and eager journalists who pre-ferred to half starve in Paris rather than draw a better wage in London. We had our share of unusual characters includ-ing one sub-editor who always carried a sword-stick, and at least twice challenged the assistant editor to a duel – with sword unsheathed in the editorial room. Another sub ran off to join the Foreign Legion (but failed the physical, and so ran back). And because it was a quirky paper, with a very strong character and tradition, even I 'inherited' an expense which I could ill afford in those days.

We were discussing the page one make-up one evening when 'Monsieur Gaston' was announced. Somebody went out to see him, and told me that he was the office masseur. The greetings from pre-war members of the staff proved that he had been masseur to my predecessor; as he told me, '*C'est la tradition, Monsieur le patron.*' The trouble was that I had to pay. Still, I felt so sorry for him that I couldn't refuse his services, because obviously he was short of clients. Most of the French needed to put on weight, not take it off. And anyway, I had little opportunity for sport at first, so massage seemed a good substitute.

Gaston came to the flat twice a week and, while I lay naked on a towel on the dining-room table, pummelled me for twenty minutes on each side. The experiment ended ab-ruptly. I like a man to be involved in his work, however hum-drum, and though I appreciated that most of Gaston's clients were ladies, I felt that his heart was not in his job when one morning, as I lay starkers on my back, he finished the front and said mechanically, '*Tournez, madame, s'il vous plaît.*'

Editing a newspaper was in itself a new and exciting challenge, though it was not always easy with the limited funds at our disposal. Then I had an idea. Many of our readers were French, and would have been cut off from British writing for the past five years. So I wrote to several old friends who had achieved fame and asked if I could buy, for very modest sums, the third – or fourth – or fifth – serial rights to some of their work. The fees I could offer were insulting – yet at a time when no one could take money out of England, they did mean that those who agreed would have a little cash waiting for them if they visited France.

Among the first to agree was Noël Coward, who carefully hid a heart of gold behind that flippant, cynical exterior. I had met him first in Leeds when I was a reporter on the *Yorkshire Post*, and he had given me a rare interview. 'Keep in touch,' he said, and I did. The result was that we printed acres of Noël's plays, stories and verse, and finally the time came when he made his first post-war visit to Paris.

A cable announcing his imminent arrival also said that I had been invited to a cocktail party being given in his honour. I arrived before him, and was swallowed up in a milling, champagne-drinking crowd. Then Noël appeared. I waved, he walked up to me and gave me a firm kiss. Well, what could I, as a trained journalist (and a good friend) do but kiss him back?

As we talked, the sycophants crushed around. Casually, I said, 'Great to see you,' adding, in a stage whisper, 'and don't forget I have some money for you.'

A master of timing, Noël looked up in his own special way, indicating that he was about to speak to the entire audience, and then announced in ringing tones, 'Wonderful, darling boy! Just put the money on the mantelpiece as usual.'

Noël was only one of the many friends who helped us out in those penniless days. Others quickly followed, and nothing gave me more pleasure than to reply in offhand fashion to cables from head office in London querying expenditure after we had produced an issue containing work by well-known contributors.

I arrived at the office one morning to find a terse telex from London, a grim reminder that across the Channel unseen overlords cocooned in austerity were watching with suspicion for any signs of the extravagance accountants seem always to associate with journalists sent to live in Paris. The message read: 'Please advise how much you paid to contributors for the feature articles in Monday's paper.'

I looked through the two feature pages. There was a very good piece by Bernard Shaw, an off-beat article on the role of modern Chinese women by Madame Chiang Kai-shek. Theodore H. White (later to become famous as the author of the 'Making of the President' books) was, like me in those days, working for peanuts in Paris, and had written a perspicacious forecast of European political developments, while Harold King had an astute analysis of future French political trends. Another political diary appeared under the name of Randolph Churchill. On the second page was the first instalment of a play by Noël Coward, an American column by Walter Winchell, and a Paris society diary by Elsa Maxwell.

Not bad for a penniless paper. Ever anxious to economise on telex messages, I replied laconically, 'Thirteen pounds regards Noël.'

The articles by Shaw and Madame Chiang were from a never-ending supply provided by PA–Reuters Feature Service, which in the main existed to sell articles to Reuters subscribers the world over. The articles had probably already earned their authors hundreds of pounds in dribs and drabs; our contribution was a small bonus of £2 a piece. Winchell came into a similar category. Who on earth would expect the ultra-American Walter Winchell's daily column to appear in 'Paris, France'? Since his column was already syndicated in hundreds of American newspapers, providing him with an almost indecent income, I was able to buy his output for $10 a week, on the understanding that I was to pick out the items suitable for Paris (and Americans in Paris) and telescope them into not more than one weekly column. Noël Coward I paid £5 for every extract – not much, but over the months it mounted up for him.

The other contributions cost nothing, not a penny – because of a curious irony. Foreign columnists writing in post-war Paris might earn good money and appear regularly in their own countries, but they lacked a local shop window. A columnist depends on contacts, and it is extremely frustrating never to be able to show those contacts the end product. Teddy White, who was based in Paris, faced just this problem – until we met. I admired Teddy very much indeed. Short, with thick glasses, dark hair, bubbling with enthusiasm, and a very good writer, he had already achieved considerable distinction for his books on China; now, in Paris, he was working for the North American News Alliance. He had an almost extravagant diligence in seeking out facts and an impressive array of contacts, but he needed a Paris platform to prove himself to them. He knew the *Continental Daily Mail* was read in every embassy and government department in Paris, and admitted frankly that *he* needed *us*: NANA, he said, would charge us a nominal subscription rate. It required no accountant to convince Teddy that we could not afford even a nominal sum. So we struck a highly satisfactory bargain: Teddy *gave* us carbon copies of the exclusives he airmailed to New York. He had his platform – and his articles were so good that they usually ended up on page 1 of the *Daily Mail*.

Before long Randolph Churchill, whom I had met at the Embassy, was writing for us under a similar arrangement. So was Harold King, the irascible but brilliant head of the Reuters Paris office, who became furious every time the Reuters office in London cut his copy. Harold had more friends in the de Gaulle camp than any other British writer, and a deep knowledge of the French political scene. He too needed to show his contacts what he had written, so he gave us carbon copies of his articles. 'Let's cut out the bloody London sub-editors,' he growled in his gravelly voice.

Then the first Paris social season burst upon the French capital, and once the Windsors had taken up residence, Paris quickly became the most glittering capital in Europe. Elsa Maxwell installed herself in a suite at the Ritz. And since Elsa disapproved of paying for hotel rooms (or anything, for that matter) she was equally anxious that Madame Ritz should have instant, visible proof of what she was getting in exchange for her bread and caviar. Her column, I must admit, was not the sort I regarded as required reading, but when ruthlessly sub-edited and cut, it did provide our readers with the sort of harmless tittle-tattle that many of them enjoyed.

Though she was a snob, and the world's most inveterate name-dropper, I will not have a word said against Elsa Maxwell. The daughter of poor parents, she was born (with an early flair for public relations) in a theatre box during a performance of *Mignon* at Keokuk, Iowa, and grew up so fat and ugly that she could say to me, 'The secret of my success is that no woman has ever been jealous of me.' Before she died in 1963 she made a living by arranging parties for the rich yearning for amusement but too busy to do anything about it themselves, or for aspiring *nouveaux riches* anxious to improve their station by a display of ostentatious hospitality. And since Elsa could always arrange the venue, and then print details in her column, there was always a free suite for her in any five-star European hotel (not to mention the *Queen Mary*).

At first, when we met, her ability to sit in the Ritz Hotel while the ex-crowned heads of Europe paid their respects, nauseated me; but then I remembered the motto that Beaverbrook had drilled relentlessly into every one of us when I worked on the *Daily Express*: 'These names make news.' It was one secret of his newspaper's phenomenal success. And Elsa Maxwell produced names by the hatful.

My comparatively precarious financial position now took a turn for the better. Day-to-day living was a problem in a sumptuous apartment staffed by a magnificent Korean cook whose enthusiasm for turning army rations into *haute cuisine* was beginning to wane. I *could* afford good French food at home occasionally, but not often; nor could I afford to patronise restaurants. Until, that is, I was given, in a sense, the honorary freedom of Maxim's.

Maxim's in the rue Royale was perhaps the most legendary restaurant in Europe. The Frenchest of French restaurants (or at least everyone from Toulouse-Lautrec onwards seemed to think so), in fact this haunt of celebrities, with its deliberately faded red plush and brass, was – surprise, surprise – at that time British-owned (though with a French chef, thank God). Nevertheless, the French had managed during the war to keep Maxim's open, serving splendid meals, presided over by the renowned *maître d'hôtel* Albert, who could always be persuaded to find a little something extra for a distinguished guest. Unfortunately he included Hermann Goering in this category, a man of roughly the same build and weight as Albert himself. Goering had liked the first table on the right as he entered the door, and Albert had done everything possible to whet the Field-Marshal's appetite on his foraging visits to Paris.

With the defeat of Germany, waiters who had long cowered under Albert's tongue-lashing (even many distinguished clients held him in awe) rushed forward with evidence of his perfidy. Maxim's prepared to be closed down, and Albert had all but packed his grip for a stay in Fresnes prison, when, with a practical if selfish gesture, some influential Britons stepped in with an offer: there would be no closure order, and the French would be persuaded to take no action against Albert, if Maxim's would agree to become the 'British Empire Club' until the end of 1945. Any British businessman anxious to open up markets in France could – if approved by the British Embassy; the George Dawsons had to wait – become a member during his stay in Paris, and thus have one restaurant where it was possible to eat and entertain at a modest cost.

I qualified on a permanent basis, until New Year's Eve

1945, so I lunched almost every day at the same table at Maxim's, and was served a set three-course lunch with *vin ordinaire* at a price well within my means – around 50p, including service, of course.

At first I was just 'another businessman' – until Marlene Dietrich came to town. She was appearing (for no salary, as usual when entertaining the troops) at the Olympia theatre near the Madeleine. It so happened that the Americans, who had asked her to sing, had no institution that could begin to match the British with their stranglehold on the one and only Maxim's. It also happened that I had met Marlene in California. A casual invitation – 'Do come and lunch at Maxim's with me!' – repeated from time to time, set the seal on my stock with the waiters, to say nothing of Albert who, with his huge, quivering jowls, could be ferociously rude, as I saw when one American tourist arrived as I waited in the bar. Albert was horrified to see that the man was dressed in 'Truman' multi-coloured summer shirt and no jacket. When he asked for a table, Albert shook his jowl, muttered that every table was booked, whereupon the luckless man, who was with his girlfriend, asked whether there would be a free table on the following day. That horrible jowl wobbled.

'Well, when then?' asked the tourist.

'We are booked up forever m'sieu,' said Albert.

Alas, all good things come to an end, and the birth of 1946 coincided with the demise of the British Empire Club. Maxim's had done its penance, and was now allowed to go public. Gastonomically speaking, that would have spelt disaster for me had I not taken precautions. The managing director of Maxim's was an affable Englishman called Keith Trevor, who had been very upset at the goings-on in France while he was fighting with the British. Any simple method of re-establishing Maxim's reputation would be more than welcome, so long as it did not cost too much.

I put a proposition to him. 'Why don't you advertise regularly in the *Continental Daily Mail*?' I suggested. 'I know it's not going to bring in any British customers, but it will have a long-term prestige effect.' I knew of course that nobody could afford to advertise in those difficult post-war months, so we hit on a happy compromise. Maxim's was to take prestige advertising in the *Continental Daily Mail* to the tune of quarter of a million francs a month, for free. This would cost *us* nothing for we carried very few advertisements, and in fact the sight of such a prestigious name might even encourage other paying clients. In return I – and Marlene and my other guests – could consume a quarter of a million francs worth of food and drink a month at Maxim's – which would not, of course, cost Maxim's anything like that amount

So when the British Empire Club closed and the new, liberated Maxim's was free to charge 'normal' prices, I was still able to sit at my usual table – only now I was actually saving 10 shillings per head, per meal, an important consideration in those days.

3

A ROSE AMONG THORNS

OUR DAZZLING ARRAY of contributors on the Paris *Daily Mail* was soon joined by another, the Duke of Windsor. He did have to be paid, but the rates were modest, despite the fact that his memoirs were a hot literary property. In England the serial rights had been snapped up by the *Daily Express*, and similar contracts had been signed in virtually every country in the world.

Once again we came into that unusual category, an English-language newspaper in a foreign country. Like our other contributors, the Duke was delighted; most of his friends in Paris were English, and like other writers, he wanted a local platform for his work.

I arranged with London for a powerful letter of introduction, whereupon the Duke asked me to lunch with him and the Duchess in the house they had rented in the rue de la Faisanderie, near the Bois.

The Duchess quickly, but politely, took charge, and I was fascinated once I had become used to the harsh timbre of her voice. She was a perfectionist, with taste, with elegance, and with determination, and had the circumstances of their marriage been less distressing, I would have described her as the power behind the throne.

Her taste, as I say, was impeccable. When the Windsors moved into the large old-fashioned house, the entrance hall was dominated by an unsightly statue of a horseman, an eyesore which could not be removed. Yet after a few weeks it seemed to have vanished. She had hidden it – disguised it – in such a manner that no one could guess the statue was still there. Of course she had the advantage of power and money. She could call on the best brains to advise her, but that does not detract from her intelligence, for she went to immense trouble to find out where the best brains were.

Perhaps because of the way the Duke had been treated, she would brook no open opposition to the theories he aired – and since, as he once told me, 'I'm not much of a one for reading', he at times talked a lot of nonsense, as most of us do. I was not the only one to see the ready smile disappear from the face of the Duchess if someone disagreed violently with her husband. In an instant her rather pinched face set, her mouth became a hard, angry line of disapproval. When Bill Patten, a gentle, charming American diplomat, objected to the Duke calling the American General Marshall a Communist – which was patently ridiculous – Patten's wife remembers that she 'happened to look at the Duchess. She was tight-lipped and cobra-eyed.' The Pattens, who were close friends, were never invited again.

Still, she was a good hostess. Those who stayed at the mill that was their country house outside Paris found the sheets ironed daily. The food was as good as any in Paris, dinner nearly always ending with the same savoury, consisting of thin strips of Canadian bacon fried crisply, then dipped in boiling molasses for a few moments, drained, and when cold served without further adornment. (The dish may still be served at the Hôtel du Palais in Biarritz, because when the Windsors stayed there, the Duchess taught the chef how to make it for her husband.)

She rarely gave a party in a restaurant without careful planning. Once, when the Duke was in England, the Duchess invited eight of us to dine at Lapérouse. Her personal table linen, silver, even book matches bearing the royal crest, had all been sent in advance to the private room in the restaurant.

Her energy never flagged. She took her French lessons with the same zeal that she collected antiques. When she heard that a couple of my amateur paintings were being exhibited in Paris (probably the organisers thought it a good idea to humour an editor) she asked to see more of my work in my apartment. I suggested lunch first, and she arrived, in sparkling spirits, at the Méditerranée at 1.30 and (according to my diary) downed two martinis before her *prosciutto é melone* and dressed crab. Though she was as bright as a button she had been out dancing until 5.30 with Jimmy Donahue, the Woolworth heir and what is known suggestively as her 'constant companion'.

She danced regularly with Jimmy, a self-confessed old-fashioned playboy, because she loved late nights and the Duke hated them – so much so that Elsa Maxwell asked the Duke one evening, in my hearing, 'Don't you get jealous, letting the Duchess go out every night with Jimmy?' Donahue was young, good-looking, rich, and Elsa was trying to warn the Duke politely that rumours were beginning to circulate in Paris. He roared with laughter, and in his special semi-Cockney accent, said, 'She's as safe as houses with *him*.' She wasn't.

The Duke's idea of a night out was a quiet dinner at Maxim's, then home to bed. But he would only go to Maxim's if he could sit at the first banquette table on the left as one entered the main *salon* (as distinct from the second, narrow dining room where in the days of *La Belle Époque* the unwritten code stipulated that a young blood must dine with his latest favourite until he had bedded her – after which he triumphantly paraded her before his friends in the main room). The table posed protocol problems because both the Windsors and King Peter of Yugoslavia, who also lived in Paris, insisted on having the same table. Peter had precedence, for though he was out of a job, he still bore the title of King (in the same way as Constantine of Greece does today), whereas the Duke was unmistakably a member of the 'ex'-club. So when Peter was dining, a discreet word would be relayed to the Duke's secretary, and presumably the Windsors would take pot luck at home.

But Maxim's was the Duke's favourite place, and it was there that I learned why he always drank the same brandy, resolutely refusing more expensive, much older amber liquid in encrusted bottles. As the meal ended Albert, his dewlaps quivering like pieces of liver, offered us his best Napoléon brandy.

'No, thank you,' said the Duke firmly. 'Let's have some Hennessey XO.'

Albert retreated with a puzzled shake of the head, and the XO was produced. As we warmed our glasses, I asked, almost idly, the reason for his preference.

'Well, Noel,' he replied, 'we always used to drink XO when I lived at Buckingham Palace, and what was good enough for me when I was King is good enough for me now.'

If the Duke decided to visit a night club, he almost always chose Monseigneur's, with its fifty or so violinists sawing away at sickly Russian-style music. The Duchess liked Monseigneur's too, and would always carefully tell each guest where he or she was expected to sit.

She was brilliant when facing up to the unexpected. One evening Barbara Stanwyck was there, and almost as soon as we arrived the music ended with a roll of drums, and an MC announced, 'We are very proud to be honoured by ze famous film star Meess Stanwyck.' After some clapping, a pretty girl simpered forward with a dozen long-stemmed roses. She made only one mistake. Sweeping past Miss Stanwyck, she deposited them in the lap of the Duchess.

As the titters rippled round the room, and I heard the MC whisper to the girl, '*Idiote*!', the Duchess, without a moment's hesitation, took the flowers across the dance floor and gave them to their rightful owner. Great cheers – for both women.

But if the Duchess enjoyed her life, the Duke on the whole seemed sad – or perhaps he was just bored. He was, so to speak, on the dole, and nobody wanted to employ him. And while it may be said that his character was flawed, and if Wallis Simpson had not come along, some other crisis might have rocked his reign, it seems a pity that no job could be found suited to his many talents.

Instead, this sandy-haired, slim man who still looked young, a man who had spent an active, hard-working youth as a highly successful ambassador-at-large, was consigned to a golden scrap heap.

Once when we were lunching alone, I asked him how he was spending the day. He had visited some antique shops with the Duchess in the morning. He was playing golf in the afternoon. 'We're dining with some people this evening,' he added, 'but I've forgotten who they are until I look in my book.'

I went away feeling very sorry for him.

The Duke and King Peter were both out of work, but another Parisian aristocrat was still very much a ruler. I met the old Aga Khan – the father of Aly – because the *Daily Mail* helped him to produce his memoirs and, though I had nothing to do with writing them, I was involved in the early approaches. I liked him. He was an outspoken self-made man. He might have been descended from Fatima, the daughter of the Prophet, and consequently the spiritual leader of the Ismaili Moslems, but when he inherited the job, the privy purse was far from full. The Aga, however, was an astute investor and made a fortune; and though he lived like a king, he (and Karim, the present Aga) have always shared out vast amounts of money among their subjects.

A hostess could spend hours working out the permutations when both the Windsors and the Aga were invited to her home. An aunt of Charles Graves (the writer, and brother of Robert Graves, the poet), was giving a party in Paris to which both were invited, and after receiving contrary advice, finally appealed to the British Embassy. According to Charles, who told me the story, the Embassy replied, 'His Highness the Aga Khan is regarded as God on earth by his many million followers. But an English duke of course takes precedence.'

The Aga's autobiography was dull, but then the only way a self-made man can make his life story interesting is to write it himself. Usually, however, such men are too busy guarding the 'made' to bother with the 'self'. The Aga's book, for all that, tended to make him a little pompous in his old age; it happens to many an 'author' who has never written anything but who finally becomes happily convinced that every word in his book is his own.

Pomposity takes different forms. I was lunching at Maxim's with Sidney Beer, the Monte Carlo bank-breaker, and the Aga was at the next table. The waiter had just brought us what I consider to be one of the simplest and tastiest first courses known to man, *oeufs brouillés à l'estragon*, the most perfect way yet invented of flavouring lightly scrambled eggs. The Aga peered through his pebble glasses, wagged a reproving finger and – with no words before and no more to follow – barked out to Sidney, 'Never eat eggs in a restaurant!'

Had this startling advice been addressed to me, I would probably have thought of a brilliant riposte the following morning. But Sidney was made of sterner stuff. With a whispered aside to me, 'Pompous old fart!', he looked back at the Aga, his face portraying a sense of deep indignation that anyone could have thought him so ignorant, and retorted, 'But I *always* bring my *own* eggs to a restaurant.'

Not all Paris meals started with such good food. The worst formal meal I ever ate was not only in Paris, but even worse, in the prestigious Hôtel George Cinq, where I had been invited by Ernest Bevin, bluff and bespectacled, who was in Paris for a Foreign Ministers' conference.

Unsmiling waiters glumly served us with tinned ham, Spam or sausages, tinned potato salad and rat-trap cheese. But before the writs for libel start to flow, it should be explained that Bevin faced a problem far more tricky than any in his talks with the Russian Foreign Minister – the danger of a rebellion among his secretarial staff, imported from London, and occupying an entire floor at the George Cinq.

'I thought they'd go on strike, and I wouldn't 'ave blamed 'em, when they saw this bloody French food,' said Ernie. 'Fish with their bloody tails stuck in their mouths!' It was apparent that the sight (let alone the taste) of *maquereaux au vin blanc* was also too much for Bevin. 'So,' he said, 'I indented for NAAFI rations for all of us, and now everybody's 'appy.'

Bevin was one of a long list of visitors who enlivened our drab lives. Everybody seemed to pass through Paris in those days, including my brother Tony, liberated from a German prisoner-of-war camp. Tony had made a record non-stop flight from England to Gibraltar in a Spitfire stripped of all its guns, which had been replaced with special cameras and extra fuel tanks. His mission was to fly secretly over North Africa and photograph possible landing sites for the proposed Allied invasion. On his way back he was forced to bale out over the Channel and was captured by the Germans after an uncomfortable few hours in the water. After more than three years in various camps in Poland and Germany he was released by the Russians and arrived in Paris without any idea that I was living there until he bought a copy of the *Daily Mail* and saw my name and title (which under French law had to be printed in each issue).

He looked very thin, so we dined at Maxim's, but where to take your kid brother after he has been cut off for years from the recurring delights of youth? It seemed to me that a nightcap at the Sphinx was called for.

The Sphinx was a remarkable institution, the best of its kind before it and similar places were closed down. Though there were girls in abundance and a fair number of small rooms in which the principal item of furniture seemed to be a bed, the Sphinx also boasted a very long and delightful bar where many a businessman popped in for a drink on his way home, with never a wandering thought in his mind. (Note the easy fluency with which I protect the reputation of a future Cabinet Minister.)

True the dozen or so barmaids were dressed in vaguely

Grecian white robes which left little to the imagination, because the girls had cleverly divided up their costumes. One wore a long flowing skirt with nothing on top, another wore a top with nothing below. At a time of national shortages it made six dresses do for twelve girls.

My favourite girl at the Sphinx – or perhaps I should be more precise and say my favourite barmaid – was a delicious little Indo-Chinese nicknamed Samsoo, who looked like an André Previn doll, with pert nose, a jet black Cleopatra bob, and capable of giving the same enthusiastic bouncy performance as that maestro of the podium. She took one look at Tony in his rags and whispered, ' 'E must be very rich to dress like that, or' – anxiously – 'very poor.'

Tony departed for London (don't ask me what happened in between) and later became Chancellor of the Exchequer, and later still, a Life Peer.

One of the next visitors was Churchill, and I was invited to lunch with him by Duff Cooper, whom I have always regarded as Britain's finest post-war Ambassador to France – a man of wit and erudition who showed me many kindnesses, and whose legendary wife Diana had all the ethereal beauty of the Madonna she once played for Max Reinhardt.

Churchill was visiting Paris privately, and Duff Cooper arranged a small lunch for him at a restaurant near the British Embassy. I was seated next to Churchill, and on our way back to the Embassy, in the faubourg Saint-Honoré, I asked him whether he could spare me a few minutes, explaining that I did not want an interview, but that, as the editor of a responsible newspaper, I would be intrigued to hear his views on the prospects facing Europe.

'Very laudable,' he grunted as, stick in hand, cigar jutting out of his mouth like a fixture, he strolled through the quickly growing crowds crying, '*Merci*, Winnie!' It was a very touching moment.

At the foot of the Embassy stairs Churchill turned to Diana Cooper and said in that gruff voice of his, almost mouthing the words, 'Pray excuse me, my dear. Mr Barber and I are going to discuss the future of Europe in my bedroom.'

Quietly I closed the door behind us. Churchill sat down heavily on the edge of his bed. Lunch had taken a long time to drink, let alone eat.

'I wonder,' asked Churchill, 'if you would be good enough to do me a small favour.'

'Of course,' I replied.

'If you would be so kind as to unlace my boots.'

I knelt down and untied the laces. With some effort, Churchill hoisted his legs on to the bed, while I awaited agog for the great man to reveal the future of our war-torn continent.

'I am most grateful to you, Mr Barber.' Churchill solemnly held out his hand. 'It has been very pleasant making your acquaintance. Good afternoon to you.'

Churchill departed. Millicent Hearst arrived, and was introduced to me at a party and we got on famously, possibly because as a 'bachelor' I could be called on from time to time to make up numbers. She was the wife (and determined to remain the wife) of the newspaper magnate William Randolph Hearst, who was living in sin with Marion Davies. I must have told Mrs Hearst that I did not seem able to have children (which was true at that time); as she frequently used words in the wrong context, I became 'good friends', as they say, with several pretty girls to whom she introduced me in those pre-pill days with the startling remark, 'At least if you like Noel, you won't have to worry, he's sterling!'

Millicent departed. Bing Crosby arrived, and I was introduced to him by Teddy Phillips – Commander Edward Phillips, at that time a confirmed bachelor of independent means, who worked with Duff Cooper at the Embassy. Very tall, slim and handsome, with a slow chuckle, he really did qualify for that hackneyed phrase 'the man who knew everyone'. Certainly, if you wanted to find the prettiest girl at a cocktail party, all you had to do was look for Teddy's head above the others, for she would be by his side.

We met at the Travellers' where Teddy had taken Bing Crosby for a drink. His visit was drawing to an end and I asked if he had enjoyed himself.

'Sure,' he said in a voice that sounded very unsure. 'Trouble is, every party I go to is American, just like back home. And anyone who isn't American, he's the Prince of this or the Count of that.'

By chance I was having a rare lunch party the next day, with Li preparing for several guests. Among them was Suzy Solidor, the singer who ran her own night club behind the Opéra, the walls of which were decorated with eighty-seven portraits of herself in various stages of undress. I had also invited Colette Mars, one of the dishiest singers in Paris; Edward Molyneux, at the height of his fame as a dress designer; and Ian Fleming who, though he had not yet invited James Bond, was a fascinating luncheon companion.

'Come and see how the poor live on expenses,' I suggested. 'They're an assorted bunch, but I guarantee there won't be a title among them.'

It is not for me to comment on the quality of Li's cooking, but the guests did not leave until 6 p.m., before which time Suzy, Colette and Bing had each sung at the piano.

Two days later Bing returned to America, leaving behind two heavy cases, with a note which read, 'Dear Noel, thanks for a swell lunch. No use taking this stuff back Stateside.'

The 'stuff' consisted of two cases of Scotch.

The Americans are the most generous people on earth, and though it is usually the spontaneous gesture that one reads about, many take infinite trouble, particularly those who share Jefferson's belief that France is every man's second country.

I was spending a week-end in Chartres, when someone

at the local post office heard me speaking English and asked for help. He had just received a food parcel from America, to which was tied a letter in English addressed to 'The Postal Chief'. The letter was from a former GI, who wanted the parcel to reach a family near Chartres which had befriended him during the war. He had forgotten their name, even that of the village, but he attached these instructions: '16 kilometres south-west of Chartres, take a narrow lane that branches to the right. After about a quarter of an hour's walk you reach a small church. The bell-ringer at the church has a young daughter and it is to this daughter that I want the parcel to go.' Under the note was a rough sketch map of the area. I took the man from the post office in my car and we delivered the parcel to the Gouin family at Unbeau.

From time to time I was invited to the South of France – a night away, which is much more exciting than an hour away. Trains and boats are unfashionable these days – the cattle trucks of the skies have taken over; but I know of nothing more agreeable than to board the Blue Train at the gare de Lyon in snowbound Paris and wake up as it rattles along the side of the sea, the mountains on the left yellow with the cotton-wool balls of mimosa, and glimpses of villas rushing past, where, even in winter, the French windows are wide open to the morning sun.

Apart from tennis and bridge, the South of France was a sunlit stage peopled with fascinating characters like Picasso, Somerset Maugham, and of course the one and only Aristotle Onassis. We met several times and, considering the difference in our resources, we got on famously. He had sudden moments of delightful simplicity, for behind the carefully fostered public image, he was a shy man who had travelled a long way since the day in Smyrna (as Izmir was then called) when his Uncle Alexander was hanged and his aunt burned to death after Kemal Ataturk sacked the city. Ari's father Socrates – brother of Alexander – was in prison awaiting the noose, but even at the age of sixteen Ari displayed his remarkable talent for wheeling and dealing. Rushing about the burning city, he discovered a large stock of whisky, then in short supply, and exchanged this with a Turkish officer for a safe-conduct pass which enabled him to reach his father's hidden fortune and purchase his freedom.

Perhaps because of his tough early life, Onassis had a mania for making detailed arrangements when entertaining the celebrities with whom he liked to be surrounded. He never left anything to chance, as I discovered when invited to a lunch party for ten on the *Christina*, which was moored in the Monte Carlo yacht basin. Sitting on deck between Lady Churchill and Maria Callas, I drank ouzo as clouds scudded overhead. A pile of blankets lay at hand, but the rain held off and luncheon was served.

Halfway through we stopped for a sorbet and a cigarette. Lady Churchill asked for a blanket. Onassis and I both jumped up. As we reached the pile of blue and white blankets, I asked him, almost mischievously, 'What would you do if it *did* start to rain?'

'Come on, I'll show you,' he replied, and after handing the blanket to Lady Churchill he took me down the main stairway – and I don't mean gangway – of the *Christina*.

There, in the dining room, with its priceless Impressionist paintings on the walls, luncheon was being served – to ten empty places. The table was perfectly laid, the white wine chilled, the fish and meat plates and cutlery had been taken away, and a duplicate set of stewards was ready to serve duplicate sorbets at a second's notice.

'They have been following us, course by course.' Onassis shrugged his shoulders. 'If it rains we just continue lunch here as though nothing had happened.'

Onassis's public adulation of Churchill was part of a mania for proving himself, for having to be *seen* to be on intimate terms with the famous. It was not enough for Ari if Churchill or some other notable accepted an invitation; the world had to know. One evening in the Salles Privées, during the time when Onassis regularly invited Churchill for free holidays at the Hôtel de Paris in Monte Carlo, I stood with Onassis watching Churchill play roulette. Alas, he cut a pathetic figure. The smooth pink baby skin was as devoid of wrinkles as a balloon, and it was not a very edifying spectacle to see the great war leader placing his chips and then, each time he lost, looking vaguely round for more – at which moment the dark face of Onassis, with its built-in smile, appeared at his elbow and he gently slid over another pile of plastic money, never to be paid for.

It was not Churchill's fault: he was an old man who did not realise what was happening; but I said to Onassis, 'He's a wonderful man, but he's so old now; he can't be very exciting as a guest. Why do you go to so much trouble to entertain him?'

Onassis never hesitated. 'Some people collect famous statues,' he said. 'I prefer to collect famous people before they become statues.'

I wonder whether he had this in mind when he proposed to Jackie Kennedy.

In the South of France I also became friendly with that wizened, bitter, brilliant master of letters, Somerset Maugham (Willie to his friends), who lived in style in the Villa Mauresque at Cap Ferrat.

It was the kind of villa in the sun that all would-be writers dream about; square and white, built round a hidden central courtyard where on warm evenings we dined under the stars. Above, a gallery ran round the four sides, with doors opening on to bedrooms, and one small flight of stairs leading to Maugham's rooftop study, a large, primly furnished office with plain white shelves along one wall containing duplicate copies of his many books, manuscripts and so on. Maugham spurned the conventional desk, but worked at a large refectory table, writing everything in longhand in exercise books, and was never on any pretext disturbed before lunch. On his left was the Gauguin painted on a glass door that he had found virtually discarded in Tahiti. At first he installed it as a large window with a view of the sea beyond, but when the colours showed signs of fading, the window was bricked up against the sun, and the glass discreetly lit from behind.

Every room housed its treasures, yet, though the house was like a jewel box of paintings, books and antiques collected from all over the world, set in grounds so splendid they advertised his wealth and fame, Willie could never control his cynicism. In the first book he autographed for me, he wrote, 'To Noel Barber from W. Somerset Maugham, in memory of his visit to the author's modest home.' On another occasion he dedicated the first volume of his collected short stories, 'To Noel with the hope that he will read volumes two and three!'

With his mouth turned down at the corners, and his face a network of wrinkles, he really did look like the Chinese mandarin that Graham Sutherland caught so brilliantly in his portrait of the bitter man. For, whereas Noël Coward's cynicism had the flippancy of a man who could say, 'The world has treated me well, but I haven't treated the world so badly either', almost everything that Maugham said had a barb to it, as though he were trying to revenge himself on a world that had used him shabbily. It hadn't, of course, but he would never believe it. The admiration of the doting public which bought thousands of his books was not enough; he felt slighted – for want of a better word – by the establishment. Wealth and fame were insufficient; he wanted honour too. He was a snob, and felt that as Britain's leading man of letters he deserved a title to his name. He had not been awarded the Order of Merit, which is limited to twenty-four distinguished living Britons, and when at lunch I commented on this, Willie retorted bitterly, 'But didn't you know that in England the OM stands for the Order of Morals?'

I was staying with Maugham when we were invited for drinks with Jascha Heifetz who was passing through Monte Carlo, and at the last moment Mrs Heifetz cancelled, telephoning that her husband had a cold.

'I wonder if he's *really* got a cold,' said Maugham angrily.

'Ah, well,' – I tried to soothe his ruffled feelings – 'you know how difficult the wives of famous men can sometimes be.'

'I should know,' Willie said bitterly. 'After all I was once married to one.'

4

THE LONELINESS OF THE
LONG-DISTANCE WRITER

WHAT ON EARTH was I doing, living it up like a lord? And what devious paths had led me to a life of penniless luxury in Paris?

Since my tenth birthday when I wrote my first love story – a graffito on a school wall reading, 'I love Kathleen Pack' (Where are you, Kathleen Pack?) – I was lucky in that all I wanted from life was to earn my living by writing; and I was not dismayed because my father regarded this childish whim with the indulgence reserved for offspring who yearn to become firemen or engine drivers. 'He'll grow out of it.'

Jack, my father, was an ambitious Yorkshireman who at the age of twenty-three was working in Denmark for Lever Brothers where he met the girl of sixteen whom he married. We lived in Hull, later moving to Doncaster when he became managing director of a sweet manufacturing firm. We were never rich, but never poor. My brother Ken and I spent most of each summer in Denmark with Mama, our Danish cousins, and our nanny, Jennie. Long, long ago. All that remains now is a series of faded snapshots.

Such as: The day I was taken a prisoner-of-war by the Germans just before my fifth birthday in August 1914. We were in Denmark when war broke out, and fired with patriotism, Jack got us on to the first boat home, luckily a Danish vessel, the *Ficaria*. A German destroyer chased and boarded us, and we were taken to Heligoland, but war in those days was more 'legal', and after three months of internment the Germans allowed the *Ficaria* to continue its journey because it was Danish and neutral.

Or: The day I nearly had to go to hospital after eating half the crop of Victoria plums on the one fruit tree in our garden; and Jack's fury at my lame excuse: I had eaten them only because I was afraid the King would come and take them away. How dim can parents be! Hadn't I just been singing the national anthem, which specifically exhorted us to 'send him Victorias'?

The post-war days of wine and roses in Denmark with Mama, who, like Titina, my Italian wife now, was so different, a changed person, the moment she set foot in her own country and spoke her own language, opening up like a plant that has been steeped in water overnight.

The hot sun-soaked sands of Bornholm, the island in the Baltic (strange how the sun always shines in remembered youth) where we played each summer, with our cousins who had strange names – Gitte, Reine, Bengt, Kai.

The day when I was perhaps twelve and (while we lived in Hull for a spell) worked for two weeks with the Hull repertory company which needed a boy for a play by A. A. Milne. My first smell of grease-paint dextrously applied by their leading man, a beautiful, young and eager actor, who later played the lead in *Journey's End* and later still killed himself because Hollywood would only type him for that one kind of character.

Music, painting, and above all reading, by flashlight under the bedclothes. Looking back, I never seem to have taken seriously the thought of earning a living as a musician (not playing an instrument was a slight handicap) or as an artist. But I did know, always, that I would write for the rest of my life.

Uncle Will, headmaster of a day school in Barry, near Cardiff, giving me my first lesson in how to be happy though married, when he surreptitiously threw his breakfast of bacon and eggs into the fire. Will was married to Jack's sister Anne and I had been sent there at fourteen for a few months of cramming in the hope of passing my matriculation (laughable paternal dreams!). Aunt Anne believed everyone should eat a good breakfast and her word was law in the house, but Will waited until she had gone upstairs, then threw his breakfast into the lighted fire. 'When you get married,' he explained sadly, 'you'll find it's much less tiring to pretend than to argue.'

The day I was walking up Tynewydd Road to Uncle Will's house when suddenly I couldn't move. Everything froze – my legs and, worst of all, my face. A strange stiffness in my face and limbs had started after I had fallen heavily during a cross-country run and cut myself badly behind the ear. I didn't know, but I was starting the spasms and pain of tetanus and during the journey north (in a reserved carriage, thank God) after the doctor told Will I should be sent home to my parents. Then the peace that came when, in our new home in Doncaster, the needle went in. By luck a local specialist had experimented during the war with revolutionary methods of treating tetanus, or lockjaw as it was then more commonly called, and pumped half a pint of horse's blood into my back. Experiment successful.

I left hospital at the very moment when Jack's brother Jim came to stay with us, and over the many weeks it took for me to recuperate, Jim gave me one of the most precious gifts I ever received. Though he could not read music, he had learned half a dozen chords on the piano, and patiently he taught them to me. In a matter of weeks I had learned to improvise. I managed to play the themes from several concertos, without music, extremely badly, and of course always changing the key to suit my modest talents. Though I never had any lessons, music has been with me ever since.

In those days it was considered immoral not to work at a steady job, so any dreams of becoming a writer had to be relegated to their proper place. Imperceptibly it was brought home to me that while writing was a wonderful hobby, it should remain a hobby – unless of course it became profitable. I wrote almost every night – articles, poems, the first pages of unfinished plays, the first chapters of unfinished novels.

Jack's typically Yorkshire attitude to writing as a career

meant many heartbreaking years of struggle for me, simply because in those days the young tended to accept parental philosophy more readily than youngsters do now. And so from the moment I decided that I wanted to become a writer, I accepted that the only way to escape from the drudgery of an office job would be to write a best-seller.

I thought this even when my first article was accepted – my very first. It was hardly a startling contribution to the world's literature. At the age of sixteen, by which time I was working in Jack's office, I had attended a Scouts' jamboree somewhere in Yorkshire and on my return typed out five hundred words and delivered them to the editor of the *Doncaster Gazette*, a Mr Bingham. The article appeared the following Thursday – and that was the moment when I was really lost, when I was as hooked as any drug addict, to writing. The next day I received a letter from Mr Bingham. Would I care to call on him to discuss the possibility of writing a weekly column on scouting in the Doncaster area?

As Mr Bingham explained at our subsequent interview, this was not a financial arrangement, but a way in which I could help scouting, and it would in a sense be my 'good deed' each Thursday. 'But if the column is successful,' he added indulgently, 'I dare say we might consider a small honorarium at Christmas.'

I ran all the way back to tell Jack and Mama. Gitte, my beautiful Danish cousin, who was staying with us, jumped up and down and screamed, 'You're famous!'

Even Jack seemed impressed, but after the euphoria had died down he asked, 'How much are they going to pay you?'

'*Pay*!' I cried. 'This is an honour! It's my Scout's duty.' Money! How could I explain that I was paid money as an office boy, that I wrote for *pleasure*. I earned ten bob a week so what more did I need?

'I don't like it.' Jack seemed doubtful. 'I know Bingham. He's trying to get something for nothing. You've heard that saying – no one but a blockhead. No, old chap, I think you'd better go back to Bingham and tell him about Dr Johnson.'

'But I can't. Suppose he doesn't want the column – *my* column –'

'He will,' said Jack.

So I had to return. I walked as slowly as possible past the Corn Exchange, down Hallgate, as far as the Mansion House, not because I was afraid, but because I was trying to think of ways in which I might earn extra money and then pretend to Jack that it was coming from the *Gazette*.

Finally I was admitted to the editorial sanctum, and blurted out, 'My father says –'

'Oh, well,' sighed Mr Bingham, with the distaste of one unused to the sordid jungle of high finance, 'shall we say tuppence a line?'

My Scout notes regaled the local juvenile population for two years. I had, during that time, written a novel and a play, both terrible, but when I became a salesman for Radiance toffee, my salary and commission helped to make me forget the *Gazette*. My new job enabled me to leave home, and this opened out a prospect of new freedom; one may love one's parents, but they can be very tiring, as my children point out to me. I went to live first in Sheffield, then Birmingham, and finally in Cardiff; I acquired a natty little car.

In those years I wrote more than a dozen books or plays, all of them bad; I lacked the help and encouragement that are like water in the desert to the thirsty writer. The unsuccessful writer who knows no other writers is as lonely as the pensioner whose neighbours never notice his existence.

In my early twenties, when I did not know a soul in the world of letters, my dreams were further frustrated by the fact that I proved to be a highly successful salesman, and was soon earning, with commission, £1,000 a year – a great deal of money in the thirties. I wrote *something* nearly every night of my life, but nobody ever saw the results, because I had no one with whom I could share my ambitions, and the only hope I could see of escaping still lay in publishing a book that would justify my leaving the world of bitter sweets.

My misery was not lessened by the knowledge that my brothers were showing every sign of being 'normal'. Ken, two and a half years my junior, was already settled in London working for a bank – obviously a steady character who would go far. Tony, who was eleven years younger than me, was still at school, but had already firmly decided to study law. He was not only intelligent, he had a sense of balance remarkable in one so young; he knew *exactly* what he wanted to do – and did it. Jack and Mama were inordinately proud of my brothers, and though I knew they loved me, I also knew they could not understand why one of their sons should be so 'difficult'.

When I went home to Yorkshire for the occasional week-end filled with dreams that *this* book would be accepted, everyone listened with genuine friendship, but with equally genuine puzzlement. It was a wonderful hobby, indeed it kept me out of mischief, but as a *living*! Jack's attitude was simple, sensible and sorrowful. 'I know how you feel, and if you were a failure it would be easier to understand, but no one can give up a thousand a year for a dream.'

Nor had he the least notion of how to go about the business of writing. 'If you weren't doing so well,' he said once, 'I'd try and help by renting an office for you to write in.'

It had to be an office, it had to be a nine-to-five job. Imagine going to an office every day to write a book! 'Well,' he added, 'you can't just stay at home all day writing, can you?'

I did not have the heart to tell him that this was just what I would like to do – get up at 5 a.m., make my own breakfast, write, or think about writing, until midnight.

In the end, after five years or so as a salesman, I did just that. I left my job and decided to try my luck in London, after proving that I could just about support myself by selling the occasional article. Jack was upset. Mama was upset too. They were both sure that I was going to become a bum. The owner of Radiance Limited, a self-made man called Philip Jackson, took it as a personal insult.

When the break came, Jack insisted that before I left to live in London, I must be man enough to say good-bye to Jackson. I agreed. My erstwhile employer, a short, silver-haired, pipe-smoking man, was standing by the fireplace in his sitting room with his false teeth, as usual, on the mantelpiece, and all he said was, 'You'll come crawling back, you little bugger.'

I did not stay long in London, and did return to Doncaster – but not to Jackson. I had been offered the chance of a job as junior reporter on the Doncaster staff of the *Yorkshire Evening Post*, on condition that I learned shorthand within six weeks. For years poor Jack had tried in vain to make me take lessons; but now that there was a *real* reason for learning, I mastered enough to qualify, mostly by sitting quietly in church and taking down sermons. After two years in Doncaster I moved on at the ripe old age of twenty-six to the *Yorkshire Post* in Leeds. I have never listened to a sermon since.

I had by now written nineteen books or plays, all of which had been rejected. Taking an average of two-hundred and fifty quarto sheets to a book, this meant that I had typed out myself nearly five thousand pages, every one of which had been thrown away. Then one Friday evening in Leeds I had a sudden thought: when I first became a reporter, I faced the same hurdle that any young reporter faces – nobody had any time to teach me the most elementary rules. Why not put together the lessons which I hoped I had learned during my two years on a weekly, an evening, and now on a daily paper? (Presumably it never occurred to me that two years was hardly long enough to qualify me for the task.)

In the coming week, I was scheduled for night duty,

starting at 5 p.m. on Sunday, a 'fireman' ready in case of any big accident, or to confirm information on the telephone. All Saturday I drafted out a rough synopsis of *Newspaper Reporting*. On Sunday evening, praying that no big news would disturb my night shift, I pounded out chapter 1 on the office typewriter. For a week I hardly stopped typing, except to eat and sleep three hours each morning, but by the time my night shift ended I had finished the book, and dispatched it to an agent called Robert Somerville, whose office was just off the Strand. On 25 February 1935, a letter arrived at the Toc H hostel where I was living in Leeds. It read:

Dear Mr Barber,

You will, I am sure, be glad to hear that we have sold your *Newspaper Reporting* to Pitmans. You will have a straight ten per cent on all sales, domestic and foreign. They did not propose an advance payment, but I have persuaded them to pay £20 on publication date on account of royalties.

Yours sincerely,
ROBERT SOMERVILLE

Bob Somerville has long since emigrated to America, though certainly not on the proceeds of my work, for I never saw another penny; nor did I deserve to. The book was so shockingly bad that Pitmans must have been mad to accept it. Yet perhaps of all the heady moments of my life, that was the single most ecstatic. I had proved to myself – and also to Jack and Mama – that I *could* write a book that was good enough to be published. I had visions over my Toc H bacon and eggs that morning of my definitive book selling for years, a legendary 'must' for those wanting to become journalists, and though that never happened, nothing can ever destroy that sunny morning in Leeds. It was a first kiss.

After that there was no stopping me – or so I thought. I moved on to the *Daily Express* in Manchester as a sub-editor on the night desk, which left me free all day to write – for if I could sell one book, why not two or three? Not so. For a while, anyway.

Jack and Mama became reconciled to my life as a journalist, though always remaining slightly surprised that it was such a respectable profession. I think Jack believed that all journalists got rolling drunk every night, and were hired and fired at a moment's notice, but now, at the age of twenty-seven, I had, they were gratified to note, settled down. Obviously I would never realise the promise I had shown of becoming a business tycoon (and I was earning much less on the *Express* than I had earned selling sweets), but they would settle for a son in a steady middle-class job. Meanwhile Ken had been promoted in the bank, and Tony – ah, *there* was a bright boy! – had passed his 'matric'. No doubt about it, he would go far.

Jack and Mama were therefore horrified when I arrived home one week-end and announced that I had decided to go abroad, on a ship sailing in a fortnight. Because I wanted to see more of the world, I had been visiting the dockyards in Liverpool on my free days, to find a cheap passage – anywhere, so long as I could get away from Manchester – and after months of effort, I found one.

I had saved up £100, and after the initial shock, Jack asked, 'Where are you going?'

This was difficult to answer, for I hadn't the faintest idea. The destination of the 5000-ton tramp had not been fixed.

'But I thought you were happy – what's the *reason*?'

I could think of only one real reason – in the very same words my own son would use to me when, at the age of twenty, he set off without a job to see India, 'I want to get it out of my system.'

There was a silence, and then Jack's face seemed to crumple, and suddenly become, for a few seconds, very old. At first I thought it was despair that his eldest was letting him down, but then I realised that it was not so. It was envy. Here was I, little older than Jack had been when he married, setting off without a care to see the world: and in all the years since meeting Mama, he had been tied by marriage, children, responsibilities to a desk, his day-to-day life broken only by a month in Denmark each year.

The ship sailed to Vera Cruz, but after three months in Mexico (which included a spell of dish-washing) I found a ship that for £1 a week took me to Singapore. I landed there in January 1938, at the very moment when the editor of the *Malaya Tribune* was about to depart on six months' leave. He was actually standing at the top of the stairs at the front of the building saying good-bye when the cable arrived saying that his replacement was not coming.

The *Malaya Tribune* faced a problem. The only possible replacement in sight was a slightly scruffy man in khaki shorts who had just come off a tramp steamer where the bathing facilities were limited. I offered to put the *Sunday Tribune* 'to bed' for no pay to see if they liked what they saw. I stayed eighteen months.

I fell in love with Singapore almost the moment we dropped anchor in the roads, joining the forest of masts of the old junks just back from the spice islands, and as the first bobbing sampans came scampering towards us, I vowed I would remain for life. Each day I stayed I loved it more, and I still love Singapore more than I did yesterday but not as much as I will on my next visit – proving my belief that in order really to love a place one must work in it.

The island was a perfect mixture of everything – palm trees bending on the blinding white beaches, the spidery fish traps out at sea, with the evening lightning flashing behind. The wet heat, the hot sun; the rain at one end of a garden while I played tennis at the other. And then the violent contrasts – insoluble traffic problems yet monkeys at the bottom of the garden surrounding the small apartment I rented; orchids growing wild on the Bukit Timah Road; patient Chinese squatting over their bowls of midday rice next to air-conditioned restaurants serving oysters flown in daily from Sydney; and above all the cross-section of bustling Chinese, languid Indians, doe-eyed Malays, and of course the pink, perspiring tuans.

After a year I married, a delightful English girl called Helen Whichello who, with an adventurous streak in her blood, had also travelled to Singapore to see the world and was working there. She loved it as much as I did – more, perhaps – and we might never have left had the British not been so stupidly misinformed about the 'impregnable fortress'. And if we had stayed? Death in Changi perhaps when the Japanese arrived – or life after a living death when they were kicked out, but still together, and still in Singapore?

Instead I listened to the people who told me time and again that Singapore, with its mighty 15-inch guns, would never be attacked, and this worried me. I did not want to miss the war that was obviously coming, not for heroic reasons, but because I still had to get a second book published (though not for want of trying) and I felt that as a journalist, I must be in the thick of the history that was soon to be written. So in 1939 we decided to leave, travelling back, with our modest savings, via Hongkong, Shanghai, Peking, then up to Harbin and thence to Manchouli where we caught the Trans-Siberian on its 21-day journey to Moscow.

Within a week of arriving in London I started work again for the *Daily Express*, but now in London. In 1940 I moved over to the *Daily Mail* group as editor of the *Overseas Daily Mail*, a weekly magazine consisting of the best of the daily paper's articles during the previous week. It gave me a chance to diversify, for I had only one deadline a week. In Singapore the head of the local radio station, John Dumeresque, had invited me to do some broadcasting, so now I could pose as an expert to the BBC, and I started broadcasting regularly. I also started writing furiously, and had two books published.

Ken and Tony were both in the forces. As a lieutenant,

Tony had manned one of the last guns to fire on the
beaches at Dunkirk and I had met him (after several days
of waiting) at Waterloo on his return. After that he was
so angry because he didn't get his second pip that he
transferred to the RAF and became a Spitfire pilot. Ken
was also in the RAF and I did not want to be the odd
man out; in 1941 I joined too, and started training as a
navigator.

I nearly did not make the RAF. Despite the shortage of
air crew, the medical was tough, and the doctors looked
askance at my age. Finally I was asked to produce a
specimen of my urine. I couldn't. Lined up with a dozen
other naked men, I pushed and coughed to no avail. I
heard a rasping voice behind me, not meant for my ears,
'He's not only ancient, he can't even pee.' Then a corporal
slithered up and whispered, 'Slip me a tanner, mate, and
I'll put half the last bloke's piss in your bottle.' The luck
of the Barbers held.

After I had been commissioned as a navigator, John
Dumeresque, who in Singapore had taught me how to
broadcast, tracked me down. I was sent on a secret mission
to America, about which I am still not allowed to write. It
lasted until early 1945. And so I saw almost every aspect
of the war – as a civilian in the blitz, followed by eight
months in the ranks, a commission as a navigator, a sudden
dash across the Atlantic in the troopship *Queen Mary*, life
in California at war but in no fear of invasion or bombs,
even a whiff of neutrality during a holiday in Mexico. Then
I returned to England in a convoy out of which we lost
five ships.

Back home, I was supposed to return to the RAF, a
prospect that appalled me, for the European war was all
but over, and the first fighter jets were on the way. I would
either have had to be retrained or more likely relegated to
a dull ground job at a remote station. I went to see the
powers-that-be on the *Daily Mail*, who were looking for
an editor for the *Continental Daily Mail* which had just
reopened as a newspaper mainly for the thousands of

British troops in Europe, with the moral backing of the Ministry of Information.

It was a race against time between two sets of initials – the MoI and the RAF. The former plodded through its paperwork. I attended conferences at the *Daily Mail* offices, to answer questions the MoI kept sending by motor-cycle messengers, culminating in one which caused Stanley Horniblow, then the editor, to ask me anxiously, 'The MoI wants to know – of course you speak French?'

This was no time for trivialities like telling the truth, for my future was at stake.

'*Oui, oui,*' I cried gaily, airing one of my two words, apart from '*la plume de ma tante*'.

'Thank God.' Horniblow sighed with relief.

Two days before the final release came through from the Ministry, I was told by the RAF to hold myself in readiness for my medical – and to report in uniform. I dashed round to the Middlesex Hospital to discover what kind of delay I could expect.

'You're lucky, sir,' said the sergeant. 'You're nearly at the top of the list. A couple of days at most.'

I knew that once I had taken my medical I would never get out. Dire measures were called for. Remembering the bribe I had paid to a corporal for a specimen of my water, I determined to see if war-torn Britain still had faith in the pound sterling. Casually I dropped ten pounds in notes on the floor – and, catching the sergeant's eye, made no attempt to pick them up.

Without a word he extracted a sheet from the pile of papers, put it at the bottom, and said without a trace of embarrassment, 'Excuse me, sir, did you say you were Pilot Officer *Barlow*? Oh, Pilot Officer *Barber*! My mistake, sir, I see you are at the bottom of the list. Sorry, sir, we won't be needing you for at least a month.'

Three days later I left for Paris.

5

SEX AND THE SINGLE MAN

IT WAS IMPOSSIBLE for Helen to come with me to Paris, for I was travelling under military orders, and I faced the prospect of living in a correspondents' mess until I found an apartment. It was this – yet another parting after life in the RAF and more than a year alone in America – that was partly responsible for the eventual break-up of our marriage; but not entirely. To lay the blame wholly on the fickle finger of fate would be untrue, for most of the blame was mine.

I could easily have written this book about the second half of my life without mentioning Helen, but that would have meant shirking the confession that, though I never beat her and we remained firm friends after our divorce, the life of a grass widower in Paris did tend to go to my head. I am old-fashioned enough to believe that marriage *should* be a sacred obligation to honour each other, but each time I met a pretty girl there was a devil tapping me on the shoulder and whispering Tennyson's line, 'Free love – free field – we love but while we may.'

I cannot deny that I have always adored pretty girls, though I remained a virgin until I was eighteen, at which time I was deflowered by a married French lady in a second-floor bedroom in the Hôtel d'Angleterre in Copenhagen. It was an ecstatic yet painful experience: ecstatic because I enjoyed it, painful because (in the fashion of those days) I was untutored, and so the climax (if the word may be excused) was attended by a certain amount of embarrassment.

Not that I was unversed in the rudimentary theories of sex. When at the age of twelve I laughingly told Mama how my scoutmaster insisted on sharing my sleeping bag during a cold camping week-end, she not only changed my troop with alacrity, but introduced me to the writings and personality of Oscar Wilde. After which she read to me Julia Ward Howe's 'Battle Hymn of the Republic', with particular emphasis on the grapes of wrath. Meanwhile Jack was warning me, long before Portnoy arrived on the scene, of the dangers of overindulgence in the grapes of Roth – so graphically that for a long time I believed asylums to be populated almost entirely by frustrated young sex maniacs.

In those days, sex was *forbidden* and *wrong*. If I plucked up the courage to interfere with an unmarried girl, her father would find out and tell my father and there would be hell to pay; and if I were bold enough to become involved with a married lady (if, that is, married ladies ever did that sort of thing), her guilt would in the end force her to confess, whereupon her husband would horsewhip me. It hardly seemed worthwhile bothering, especially since in those days I played tennis all summer, rugger and squash all winter, and took a cold bath every morning.

But then I went to Copenhagen. We had been going there every year, but this time I was alone. Mama had gone ahead to Bornholm, the Baltic island seven hours by sea from the Danish capital. Jack wanted to sail from Hull and take advantage of the longer sea voyage. I went via Harwich, and was to wait a couple of days at the Hôtel d'Angleterre until Jack picked me up.

I know of no more pleasant veranda than the one in front of the d'Angleterre, its bright awnings shading the small packed tables from the sun, shining on the large square with its plane trees and the opera house on one corner. I was sitting there drinking coffee when a lady in her late twenties asked if she could sit at my table, every other one being occupied. She was French but spoke English with a delightful accent, and it transpired that she, like me, was staying at the hotel, by chance like me on the second floor.

Over coffee she told me that she was married and waiting
for her husband who would be arriving in two days. Her
name, she told me, was Natasha, which I thought very
exciting. Indeed, I found it hard to stop staring at her; she
was so beautiful, with hair almost blue it was so black.
Though I cannot remember the colour of her eyes, I do
remember thinking that I had never seen eyes so large.
'That's my touch of Russian blood,' she laughed.

She seemed so interested in me, so understanding, that
I put all thoughts of horsewhips behind me, and asked her
to accompany me to the Tivoli that evening. Once there,
she prettily invited me to dinner at Nimb's, one of Mama's
favourite haunts, with a balcony overlooking the Tivoli,
and after dinner we strolled back to the hotel through
Stroget, the collective name for the succession of narrow
shopping streets leading from the Town Hall to the
d'Angleterre.

In the lobby she suggested, 'Would you like a last drink
in my room? I have a thing about paying bar prices, don't
you?', adding, 'And if it would make you more comfortable
– since our rooms are so close – slip on your dressing gown.
By the way, what's your name?'

'Jim Conrad,' I blurted out. Why? Well, on the way
from London to Copenhagen I had started reading Conrad's *Lord Jim*, a yarn which pressure of events forced me
to leave unfinished in the Danish capital. But when the
lady asked my name I had, with visions of horsewhips,
cried, almost without thinking, 'Jim Conrad.' (Better safe
than sorry.)

I dashed back 'to slip into something more comfortable'
as they say in the movies, for I may have been a virgin,
but I knew a good thing when it was thrust under my nose,
and a few minutes later I knocked on her door, looking
anxiously up and down the corridor for any house detectives. All I remember of the room was a shadowy, out-of-
focus background of flimsy pastel blue material – nightie,
panties, dressing gown, lace pillows, perhaps. It still re-
minds me of one of those expensive boxes in which a

fragile chocolate egg reposes in a bed of frilly material. But now instead of an Easter egg there lay in it an almost perfect reproduction of Manet's *Olympia*.

This was no time for dallying (or so, in my ignorance, I thought), and with true British verve I pounced on her. It is not a pretty word but really the tempestuous quality of my ardour brooks of no substitute. Within a matter of minutes my initiation ceremony was concluded and (still haunted by thoughts of husbands and/or house detectives) I made tentative proposals to leave. At this the lady sat up in bed, looked at me witheringly, and uttered a sentence I will never forget.

'*Mais, c'est un crime!*' she breathed in disbelief. '*Vraiment, c'est un crime.*'

There was only one thing to do – bolt for it, hide in my room and hope I would never see her again. But then I had second thoughts. Why was it '*un crime*'? Was she already overwhelmed by guilt at betraying her marriage vows? Surely not. Come to think of it, she had even egged me on. It couldn't be *my* fault – for it never entered my head that she had expected the same satisfactory climax to the adventure that I had so rapidly achieved. Scarlet-faced I mumbled 'Sorry', but as I put my hand on the door knob, she suddenly smiled.

'Let me explain to you,' she said.

I spent the night with her. I spent all the next day in bed with her. And the whole of the next night. And the following day until 2.50, and then I only got up because she was leaving at 3 p.m. to meet her husband. I helped her with her luggage and then got into bed – my own bed.

I was still asleep around 11 the next morning when Jack arrived. 'You don't look too chirpy,' he said, puzzled, for I have always been an early riser. 'Change in the hour, eh?'

The sequel might have been embarrassing. No sooner had we arrived on Bornholm and joined Mama at Dam's Hotel in Ronne, the largest small town on the island, than a pretty voice trilled, 'Jeem! Jeem!'

She was sitting in a corner of the garden with her husband, and I would have thought that shame or embarrassment might have forced her to feign ignorance of my presence; but no, she insisted on waving me over, and with the wide-eyed innocence of a pure and loving wife, introduced me to her husband, 'Mr Jeem Conrad helped me so much with my luggage and a taxi at the hotel.'

Fortunately she did not ask to meet Mrs Conrad – which might have mystified Mama.

I have always been old-fashioned in my attitude to sex. Firstly, I enjoy it enormously in an age when it seems to be going out of fashion; secondly, I have always found it doubly enjoyable when coupled with love, emotion, entanglement. This is not to say that on occasions I have not enjoyed the one without the other; but I have never subscribed to the philosophy of Kemal Ataturk, who, when asked what appealed to him most in women, replied briefly, 'Availability.'

Nor is it for me to say that the lessons so charmingly given in my crammer's course in Copenhagen were well learned. Yet another French lady made a remark that would have pleased my original mentor. I had driven over the Simplon, along the sunlit Rhône valley until it burst upon what Byron called 'the crystal face' of Lake Geneva, and the exhilaration, I suppose, helped entice me into the arms of a stranger in the Beau Rivage at Lausanne. This time, the lady rewarded me with a very pretty sentence, '*Merci, chéri, pour ta patience.*'

There are times when only a 'neutral' can say no to a bizarre invitation. In the lush, tropical surroundings of Singapore during the early days of 1938, I was invited to dine with His Highness the Sultan of Johore. The Sultan – Ibrahim to his friends – had one passion in life: girls. Indeed it was rumoured that he had regular injections of bee stings so that he could enjoy his hobby to the full. Until the spring of 1938, the Sultan had been in the habit of spending evenings at the Happy World in Singapore, a barn-like structure filled with taxi dancers waiting patiently to be hired at ten cents a dance. For this modest sum, one could gyrate sedately to the music of a slow or medium foxtrot (any faster tempo made for excessive sweating in the tropical heat) in the arms of a waif-like Chinese. For a little more, they gave a little more.

Ibrahim was every inch a sultan – hair of iron grey, a tall, commanding presence – but soon his peccadilloes embarrassed the stuffy British so much that the Governor, Sir Shenton Thomas, banned him from entering Singapore after dusk. Thomas could not prevent the Sultan asking girls to visit him in Bukit Serene, his ornate palace in Johore Bahru, across the Causeway, nor could he stop the Sultan from discreetly importing an occasional favourite from abroad – which he did while I was in Singapore in the shapely figure of Lydia Hill, a London cabaret dancer.

Inevitably a free-lance photographer snapped the two of them together, and prepared to send a print to London and New York. This is where I came into the picture. I had arrived recently in Singapore; this was while I was temporary editor of the *Malaya Tribune*. I had been presented to 'HH' only briefly (I had very little social life as my first pay day had not arrived and my wardrobe consisted of only two pairs of khaki shorts, two white duck suits, and three or four shirts). When the photographer took the offending picture, the Sultan had phoned the paper, was switched through to me, and couched his request in simple terms: 'I want that picture destroyed!'

This was no time for defending the freedom of the press. I knew the photographer, and in a country where every man's price is worn on his sleeve, there was no problem. 'You pay me twice what the *Mirror* in London would and the photo is yours,' said the Chinese photographer.

The Sultan was so delighted that he invited me to a bachelor dinner at his palace in Johore, where I dutifully presented myself with a dozen or so other males. The dinner was excellent, though I do not recommend eating off gold plate, as the food tends to cool quickly. (For those who might ponder on the possibility of nicking even the smallest gold coffee spoon, there was a stalwart footman behind each diner's chair.)

The meal over, the Sultan clapped his hands, the white, gilt-edged double doors opened, and in flocked a twitter of pretty Chinese, Filipino, and Malay girls, chattering like starlings. They had all come from the Happy World, but had been completely transformed by the opulent nature of their surroundings.

'Mr Barber, you are the guest of honour,' announced the Sultan. 'Please, you have the first pick.' Without hesitation I plumped for a Filipino girl, well known as a hermaphrodite, and for long one of the Sultan's favourites. I had of course no idea where to go (though I knew what to do), and I must have looked naïve, standing there, a newcomer unversed in the ways of the 'mysterious Orient'. I was certainly unprepared for the Sultan's next remark.

'Well, come along, Mr Barber; we are all waiting, you know,' said the Sultan testily. 'Can't you count? Can't you see there are two girls each?'

But enough of these brief encounters. In Saigon a friend lent me his wife for a week, and this was a very different experience (and not so sordid as might at first be imagined), for the circumstances were unusual.

One of the *garçons de bureau* at the *Daily Mail* office in Paris had been called up for his military service. Gaston was in his early twenties, already married with a son, and was sent to Indo-China, where he joined HQ staff in Saigon. When I decided to visit the city during a holiday to research a series of articles, I naturally dropped a note to Gaston, telling him the date of my arrival at the Hotel Continental.

I loved Saigon, then one of the most entrancing cities of the East, a French-made Paris gaudily overpainted by Gauguin; in those days it was the last resort of yesterday in the China of tomorrow. The heart of the city was like a pleasant provincial French town, its main tree-lined boulevards almost labelled 'made in France'. The pavement cafés boasted the same advertisements – and the same ashtrays – for Dubonnet and Cinzano as any French boulevard café; Simcas, Renaults and Citroëns swerved with French éclat across the place Pigneau and down the boulevard de la Somme; yet always behind the thin Frenchified veil lay China, epitomised by the sullen, broad Mekong River, so that one was living in two worlds.

The first night Gaston came to dine with me at the Arc en Ciel in Cholon, one of the finest Szechuan restaurants in all Asia, and told me that he was leaving the following day with his general for a conference in Hanoi. Would I like to borrow his small flat just off the rue Catinat? He seemed to hesitate, as though trying to tell me something, but (perhaps because I was the boss?) was nervous. Finally he blurted out, 'I have a wife in the flat!'

'Lucille?' I had met his wife. 'How the hell does a conscripted *poilu* manage to get his wife out to Indo-China?'

'Well, it's not Lucille,' he said.

I had visions of a broken marriage, but then he enlightened me.

'I bought her for ten thousand francs,' he explained sheepishly, 'for two years. You know me, *patron* – I love Lucille, but a man gets fed up without a woman around the house. It's much better than going out and picking up girls.'

Intrigued, I asked for details. It appeared that hundreds of French soldiers stationed behind the lines had married Annamite or Thai girls, exquisite pale yellow flowers from the rich rice valleys between Tonkin's Red and Black rivers. The marriage was proper and binding for two years, but at the end of that time – which coincided with the term of conscription – there was an automatic divorce. For centuries girls in the area had been sold in marriage for a buffalo, a few sheep, or maybe even a bolt of cloth. It had been a trifling matter to adjust the duration of the contract to suit conditions of modern warfare.

'You're not angry, *patron*?' asked Gaston.

Not at all. A blind date can be great fun – providing you keep your eyes open.

Gaston's flat was small and cosy. Mei Ling was seventeen and beautiful, with all the passive gentleness of the Orient, where women still give a man the impression that he is actually a human being, and not merely a robot whose sole task is to work hard and provide money in return for a regular ration of ecstasy. The beautiful little Mei Ling gave me – and it was a gift – a very happy week of life.

6

THE NAKED TRUTH

ONE POPULAR FEATURE in the *Continental Daily Mail* was our daily diary, written under the pseudonym of 'Paul White'. It was not an Elsa Maxwell-type record of social trivia, but more, I hope, in the manner of Peterborough in the *Daily Telegraph*. Men like Teddy Phillips produced many excellent stories, and Teddy White produced political scoops. On the social side one of our best contacts was Suzy Solidor, the singer who was the rage of Paris.

Suzy handled the male guests in her night club with impeccable charm, courtesy and enthusiasm, but I doubt if a single one ever snuggled between the sheets with her, unless Suzy did it for a dare. The appeal of those broad shoulders, that well-known swaggering gait, and above all the husky, gritty, sexy voice was never levelled at the male members of the audience, but was directed with the deadly accuracy of a laser beam toward the most attractive women.

Suzy liked girls. I realised it, of course, the moment I met her in the summer of '45. I do not know why she liked me; perhaps, though I may be unfair to her, our friendship was based on the fact that everyone in the Paris entertainment world needed help in the first flush of liberation and I, without any pressure from her, found that her night club yielded many incidents for those on the newspaper who wrote our daily diary.

But I hope there was more to it than that. I was painting a great deal and tried, in vain, to produce a portrait for her gallery. I was also trying to write songs, tapped out on the grand piano I had hired, and Suzy had one song suitably arranged so that she could sing it. We enjoyed the happy relationship of two brothers.

All the same, when the lessons of sex discrimination are driven home too forcibly, they can lead to acute embarrassment, and it was a mistake to spend the week-end with Suzy and some of her friends at her country retreat half an hour from Paris. It was a picture-postcard cottage, with rambler roses that really did cover the front of the house, and with a small garden, mostly lawn, at the back, surrounded by an abnormally high hedge.

'It makes for privacy,' explained Suzy, 'for in this beautiful summer weather we always sunbathe in the nude.'

I was the first guest to arrive, followed shortly afterwards by a stunning Jacques Fath model with hair as black as the ace of spades. By dinner all six guests were present. I was the only male.

The old cottage suffered from one drawback: the only way from my attic bedroom to the single upstairs loo lay through one large bedroom which Suzy had made by knocking down several walls, and in which she had installed several beds. In view of this I was given first opportunity to 'brush my teeth' before retiring. But the wine had been flowing, and in the middle of the night I had to get up. Quietly I crept downstairs. Gently I opened the dormitory door, afraid of waking the others. I need not have worried. Several of the beds were empty, but three were occupied, each by two ladies, fast asleep and blissfully wrapped in each other's arms.

Sunday afternoon, after an excellent *gigot* and some chilled Beaujolais, was perfect for sunbathing. It was my turn to wash up, but I could hear a great to-do in the garden, and finally Suzy's voice, 'Noel! *Tu as fini? Où est tu?*' The kitchen had no window overlooking the garden, but the pantry did, and I took one peep. Six nude ladies in sunglasses lay stretched on their backs on Lilo-style mattresses. The raven-haired beauty was exactly as I had imagined her.

Yet I could not join them. I did not have the courage.

I have always felt that men look ridiculous in the nude, and the thought of nonchalantly strolling on to the lawn, so conspicuously different, started a sweat of apprehension. Shamefaced, I muttered that I had taken too much sun the previous week-end, and retired for a snooze to my monastic cell.

I fared much better when attending my first nudist party, which was held in the winter of 1941 in the unlikely surroundings of an old house in Shoot Up Hill.

It was in fact the annual dinner dance of the British National Sun and Air Association, the meal and dance being preceded by a nude ping-pong tournament. The *Sunday Dispatch* (for which I worked at week-ends) had arranged for me to be invited – the only non-member – following reports that British troops were using the society for indiscreet purposes (reports which I found to be without foundation).

I was greeted by a lady in a dressing gown who opened the front door furtively. But when I identified myself, she smiled and in a tone of relief said, 'Of course, sir. Our secretary is waiting for you in the front office.'

She was indeed. Her back to a blazing fire, legs akimbo like any bishop, she greeted me with a manly handshake and a hearty, 'Welcome, Mr Barber. As you will find out, we have nothing to hide.' Considering that she was wearing nothing but a pair of shoes, I could hardly dispute her words.

Before joining the festivities, I asked her several questions, which she answered willingly. I was puzzled by the date of the event, for a nude dance in mid-winter seemed a little ill-timed for a society dedicated to the sun.

'Nonsense, my dear Mr Barber,' replied the secretary. 'A club is a club – and we have to plan ways of keeping our members together in the slack season. Just like a tennis club, Mr Barber – you must have your winter functions, or the club will die.'

'But in the altogether?'

'The *nude*,' she corrected me. 'I know what you are thinking. Why not have a jolly evening in some café in the West End, eh?' She paused just perceptibly. 'Don't you think that could be a mite embarrassing? After all, most of our members have never seen each other with their clothes on.'

My questions answered – and she had made many sensible points – she scrawled my name on a large buff envelope, handed it to me, and seeing that I was bemused, explained pityingly. 'For your money and keys. After you've undressed upstairs and taken a shower, you can leave the envelope here with me for safekeeping. And, oh,' she added as I made for the door, 'there is one concession. As we are dancing, the ladies will be wearing shoes, and you can keep on your socks.'

'Socks?'

'Splinters, Mr Barber, the possibility of splinters when you're dancing.'

One small idiosyncrasy intrigued me during the evening. While dancing with a genuine redhead, I noticed that several of the men wore a strip of white material knotted round the wrist. I took it to be some kind of status symbol, possibly signifying membership of the committee. When I had danced the last waltz, said good-bye to the nubile redhead and put on my trousers, I asked the lady secretary to enlighten me.

With an almost withering look, she said, 'We *are* in the depths of winter, Mr Barber! I wonder if you could suggest any other way for a man with a cold to carry a handkerchief.'

Since then I have been asked the invariable question, 'Were there any pretty girls there?' There were, particularly two girls in their early twenties with splendid figures. I was drawn against one in the doubles ping-pong tournament, and she reprimanded me after I had lost. 'You could have won if you had only concentrated more.'

A second question has always followed the first. With pretty girls besporting themselves among the fifty or so

members, was I not afraid of – well, ahem – ah – well, of
displaying more interest than my attendance in a purely
professional capacity warranted? Or as one vulgar journalist put it, 'Did they get a rise out of you?'

The answer, mysteriously, is no. I was terrified when I
entered the room and one of the naked nubiles, in a
courtly, welcoming gesture, approached me and introi-
duced herself. How nature arranges these matters so cir-
cumspectly is beyond me. Nothing untoward happened,
and once I had realised that any fears were groundless, I
enjoyed myself immensely. I danced cheek-to-cheek with
pretty girls until 2 a.m., and my spirits never drooped –
though fortunately everything else did.

Of course it was rather different when I peeped out of
the pantry window at the black-haired Jacques Fath model
stretched out on her back on Suzy Solidor's lawn.

7

THE GENTLE ART OF
MINCING WORDS

I NEEDED MORE money. Since man cannot live by bread alone, even when supplied free by Maxim's, I had to find an alternative source of revenue to supplement my salary. It was not that I disliked the free food at Europe's most famous restaurant, but occasionally I yearned for a change for the worse. Much though I savoured my *sole Albert*, I missed my sausage and mash, and while *pâté en croûte* has its points, so has a pork pie.

In London I had supplemented my income from the *Overseas Daily Mail* by supplying food (for thought) for the insatiable appetite of the BBC, but now I was too far away. Nor did I have the inclination (at that time) to write any more books.

In the end I decided to try and win some of the glittering prizes offered in the American magazine market. I had no means of knowing if I would succeed, but at least I had an organisation behind me capable of absorbing some of the drearier chores of writing – research, typing, telephoning. And my position as editor carried enough prestige in Paris for me to ask for help from outside sources. If I thought of an interesting subject, I could sometimes arrange a free air ticket, because as editor I could at least guarantee that the article would be published, a fact which public relations officers, so often disillusioned by unfulfilled promises, were quick to appreciate.

Despite all this help, the 'American experiment' was at first a disaster. In twelve months I sold not a word, simply because I did not realise that even though I was writing in my own tongue, I still had to choose the words in a different way. Shaw was right; the Old and New Worlds *were* separated by a common language.

Yet, though I received no cheques, many letters from editors encouraged me to try again. I did – with a brain wave. Since I could not produce the style of writing required, I would try to compose an article of five thousand words containing as few words of mine as possible.

The title tells all: *'Drinking My Way Round the World'*. I dictated letters to a score of hotels I had patronised over the years, and from each I requested the recipe of their most famous drink. The magic word 'Editor' at the foot of my letters ensured speedy replies, and when the last had reached Paris, I stuck each recipe, unchanged, on a separate sheet of paper, prefaced each one with a brisk 'I was there' anecdote, had the result neatly typed, and posted it to New York.

Within two weeks *True* magazine bought it, qualifying me for an entry in the *Guinness Book of Records* as the world's first writer to be paid $1,000 for an article that appeared without one word of his own. *True* magazine was so entranced by the recipes for delicious drinks written out by public relations officers, that it threw away all my anecdotes, even my introduction, substituting a paragraph, 'Noel Barber is a world traveller who has collected . . .' This was followed by the recipes, without a PRO word changed. The hotels were delighted – La Réserve at Beaulieu even offered me a week's free stay. And though I missed my anecdotes, which I filed away in case I ever wrote this book, I saw no reason for crying all the way to the bank.

As so often happens, one stroke of good fortune quickly follows another. Hardly had I spent the $1,000 from *True* when I met Teddy Phillips at the bar of the Travellers'. He was with his cousin Ivar Bryce, who had just married an American girl, and we ended up lunching at the same table. When Bryce realised that I was a journalist, he mentioned in passing that his bride had given him as a wedding present a major share of the stock (or maybe all

the stock) in a news agency called NANA – North American News Alliance. Had I ever heard of it?

Of course I had – shades of Theordore White! But it
was not until after the *fraises de bois* that Bryce asked me
casually if I could recommend a Paris-based journalist who
might write a weekly airmail column for the agency. 'You
know, something to titivate our subscribers in small towns
– give them a picture of Gay Paree in quotes.'

I knew just the man, but at this stage merely promised
to look around. One of the fatal mistakes in journalism is
to make airy-fairy promises to people who do not know
your work. You are immediately suspect.

I dashed back to the rue des Saints-Pères and started
telephoning contacts – in itself a hazard in Paris, where
the ladies working on the exchange always seem dedicated
to the frustration of subscribers with a zeal that could
surely be put to better use.

I managed to speak to a dozen 'old faithfuls' who, after
prodding, dictated a few items to me, then presumed on
the friendship of men like Harold King who supplied me
with a few political titbits.

Li cooked me a quick bite of supper. Then I typed out
two thousand words of my first 'Continental Diary'.

The next morning I split a bottle of champagne at the
Ritz Bar with Ivar Bryce and said, 'Read this.'

'*Exactly* what I want! Who wrote it?'

'Noel Anthony.' The name came off my lips as quickly
as 'Jim Conrad'. However, teasing a possible benefactor
is stupid, so I added quickly, 'It's a name I use occasionally.
I wrote it.'

Ivar has long since severed his connection with NANA,
but in early 1976 I was dining at the Empress in London
and he was alone at the next table, so we joined forces.
As Negri, the greatest restaurant manager in England,
fussed over my special *café filtre*, Ivar and I talked of old
times, and he asked, 'I wonder what happened to that
diary we dreamed up in Paris?'

'It's fine,' I replied cheerfully. 'I posted it yesterday.'

For though I have occasionally had to delegate the writing to a colleague during trips abroad, Noel Anthony remained on the NANA payroll for nearly thirty years.

I never worry much when someone with intelligence suggests changing my words, or even deleting a few paragraphs, though I do like to know what is going on, especially since the never-to-be-forgotten day in Singapore when some words of mine were changed while I was at lunch. It taught me a lesson I have never forgotten: Never give notice of dismissal to *a man who has the last word*. Pay him off and fire him on the spot. As editor of the *Malaya Tribune*, I gave notice to the head proof reader because of the large number of literals. I disliked dismissing him, for he was an Asian with a large family, but he was just not capable of correcting proofs – a key duty on a newspaper where compositors could not speak English and set the type by rote. So the head proof reader had to go. But, to be kind, I explained to him that I would give him a week's notice, as it might be easier for him to get another job while still employed. That unpleasant chore over, I repaired to the Swimming Club for a dip and a curry tiffin.

The *Malaya Tribune* cost five cents in those days; but by the time I returned to the office around 3 p.m., the price had soared from five cents to fifty dollars a copy. For those lucky enough to find one.

Knowing the compositors would not spot what he was doing because they could not speak English, the wily proof reader had taken his revenge by deleting a headline on the front page and substituting in large black type the words:

FUCK BARBER

8

SOMETHING OF VALUE

IN A WAY I lived a double life in Paris, for though the bright
lights shone for me through many a night, I greeted other
dawns by setting up my easel at a street corner as I indulged
in one of my greatest, if least successful, loves: painting.
By chance I became an honorary member of the magic
circle of Parisian painters – artists like Dufy, Utrillo, Léger,
Vlaminck, Natalie Gontcharova, Michel Larionov, Marc
Chagall. The moments I spent in their company were some
of the happiest of my life.

Since I was interested in painting, one of the first things
I did when I arrived in Paris in 1945 was to look around
for a good art critic, and I found one in Barnett D. Conlan,
highly respected, a pillar of rectitude, and a fount of
wisdom. He introduced me to several painters, among
them Schwarz-Abrys, who did not rank with the great
masters, but was a very talented and exciting artist.

'Come and paint with me,' said Schwarz. A restless man
with an aggressive pointed beard and eyes that were never
still, he waved away my excuse that I had to be at the
office at 10 a.m. 'No problem,' he cried. 'I always start
painting at six in the morning.'

So started my double life. A couple of mornings a week
I rose at 5.30, drove to Ménilmontant (Chevalier's old
quartier) and picked up Schwarz. We looked for the crook-
edest, most twisted streets we could find, and started
painting. Around nine o'clock I drove back to the rue des
Saint-Pères, had a bath, breakfast, changed personality
and drove or walked to the office.

Painting with Schwarz was an experience never to be
forgotten. He had an answer for any situation. If a crowd

gathered round, Schwarz always asked if anyone wanted
to buy. 'Standard rates! Fifty francs a square centimetre,'
he cried. Once when an onlooker took him at his word,
he whipped out a knife, and sliced off a third of a canvas.

In those days, he did not sell many of his paintings, with
their sombre street scenes and tormented skies. Yet he
lived like a king, as I discovered one morning when pelting
rain kept us off the streets. Gathering up a dozen or so
canvases in cheap frames from his tiny studio, we set off
for the butcher, the baker, the candlestick-maker. To each
he offered to barter a painting in return for groceries,
meat, coal, wood, or a future supply of bread.

Schwarz also bartered his finished paintings for tubes of
paint, brushes, canvas, and soon I was bartering too, for
I was hard pressed to find money for canvases that were
often thrown away. No one wanted to trade *my* canvases,
but I had something worth its weight in paint.

It so happened that a top director of Maison Lefranc,
which produces everything an artist needs from easels to
turpentine, had a maniacal obsession with football – and
no real interest in paintings. When Schwarz mentioned
that I received tickets for all the big international games,
my materials problem was solved. Until that moment I
had given these tickets (which I paid for, and which were
in addition to those required for the sports staff of the
paper) to friends; after I met 'Monsieur Lefranc' he never
missed a single big match. I never posted the tickets; I
delivered them personally at the huge Lefranc warehouse,
and as he drooled over them, his henchmen were stocking
up the boot of the car with loot.

Curiously, the knowledge that I would never be a good
painter helped me to enjoy painting all the more. To me
it was a selfish pastime, in which the only person I had to
please was myself; I never had to move on to the stark
realities of the professionals, as I do in my profession as a
writer, where the main yardstick by which I can measure
any modest success must be the ability to live by writing.
As a writer, I must accept the judgement of a publisher or

editor who may be a total stranger, but in the wonderful,
exciting world of the Sunday painter, I would sweat all
morning, and if everything went wrong, throw the canvas
away, start again, and somehow, in the end, occasionally
reach the magical moment when I produced a painting that
pleased *me*, if no one else.

Schwarz and Barnett Conlan introduced me to other
painters, and I became so intrigued with their lives that I
started writing a series of scripts, 'Painters in Paris', as
seen through the eyes of an English amateur; these I
broadcast once a week on the French radio.

One Sunday morning Schwarz and I went to see Utrillo
at his home at Le Vésinet, a few miles outside Paris on the
road to Versailles. It was an extraordinary meeting –
extraordinary because before lunch Utrillo painted a canvas for me in exchange for a bottle of wine.

The great (if alcoholic) painter, renowned (amongst
other subjects) for his wonderful Montmartre scenes, lived
in an ugly pink stucco villa, with a tasteless garden, in
which fountains and terracotta statues jostled each other.
When Schwarz had suggested going to see him, the most
I hoped for was to absorb a little atmosphere for the
following week's broadcast. This, I knew, would be easier
if Madame Utrillo were otherwise engaged: Utrillo's wife,
Lucie Valore, exercised a powerful influence over her
weak and wayward husband. Rightly, she watched him
like a hawk, determined that he would never return to an
alcoholic ward. But Schwarz promised to walk her up and
down the garden while I talked to Utrillo.

Though only in his sixties, he was a frail creature in blue
denims and carpet slippers, but he talked quite lucidly
until, after peering out of the window to make sure his
wife was out of the way, he whispered, 'I'm thirsty! Could
you get me a glass of wine?'

At first I refused, but then the shabbily dressed figure
blinked his rheumy eyes and added something that made
me change my mind. 'I want to paint,' he said pathetically,
'and I can't paint unless I have just one drink.'

I nipped down to the kitchen, poured out a glass, took it upstairs. Almost immediately Utrillo started work on a small Montmartre scene, copying it from a postcard. A few more glasses followed – and then, when the painting was finished, something else happened. Tearfully, Utrillo kissed me on both cheeks, thrust the small wet canvas under my nose and cried, 'I've had such a wonderful morning. This is yours – a gift to a good friend.'

Much of Utrillo's work was copied from postcards or photographs, though in his earlier days he had painted in the streets of Montmartre. But as he drank more and more, his family persuaded him to keep away from the bars of the Place du Tertre which he loved so much. Yet Utrillo could transform the drabbest postcard into a painting of beauty – not always, but more times than not.

One of his friends, Kees Van Dongen the portrait painter, told me how they had once spent a few weeks together on the French Riviera. In the warm summer Utrillo was seized with a passion to work and for three months hardly stopped painting. When finally the 'holiday' ended, the canvases were sent to Paris in crates.

Then came the moment at Le Vésinet when the nails were prised out and excited friends waited to see how Utrillo had coped with the problem of the harsh, different Mediterranean light. The paintings were spread out – and every one was a snow scene of Montmartre.

Someone else gave me a painting – Fernard Léger, so much a Frenchman that even after living in America for four years he could not speak a word of English. Léger was more than French, he was Norman. In every way a big man, he had the grizzled, unsmiling face of the peasant who takes a swig of Calvados before breakfast to keep out the cold. Léger's home was 'in a village', as he once explained to me, 'half-way between the cheeses of Camembert and Pont l'Évêque.'

He did, however, have a studio in Paris, at the top of a winding circle of narrow stairs in Montparnasse. It was

small and dirty, for, as though rebelling against the ma-
chines which were, so to speak, the stock in trade of
his paintings, he refused to have a regular cleaner, and
depended for heating on an ancient stove with a pipe
leading to a hole in the ceiling, with a heap of *boulets*, the
typically French egg-shaped lumps of pressed coal, nearby.
I was accorded one special privilege of friendship – I used
occasionally to light the fire in his iron stove, and one
morning after breakfast at the Deux Magots he grunted,
'You can start the stove while I sweep up.'

Léger's idea of cleaning a room was to sweep anything
that wouldn't burn into a corner and hope for the best.
Anything that would burn went straight into the stove.
And that particular morning after the fire was going well,
he gathered up a dozen or so gouache studies he had
painted for a picture, and lifted the top off the stove.

'You can't do that,' I cried, horrified.

'Why not?' he replied gruffly.

Without thinking, I blurted out, 'Well, at least let me
have one as a souvenir, instead of just burning them.'

For a moment he hesitated, then he said very quietly,
'Do you *really* want one?'

I felt a little embarrassed and said nothing. He muttered,
'Well, frankly, I don't think they're good enough,' and
threw them in, and they went up in flames.

About a week later, a small package arrived at my
apartment. It was an exquisite oil, with a note from Léger
reading, '*Cher ami*, this I think is a *little* better.'

No two men could have been more different than Léger
and Chagall. The gentle, almost timid Russian first came
to France without any thought of staying. But, as he told
me, 'The minute I arrived in France I found that so long
as I did not get into trouble I was allowed to do exactly as
I wanted. So I decided to stay.'

Chagall was living in Vence when we met, and he came
down the steps of the house to greet me, eyes twinkling,
a cherubic face beneath grey hair like strands of tangled

wool. He was wearing a bright blue shirt, red velvet jacket, grey trousers and carpet slippers. Madame Chagall was British – tall, with dark hair and a sudden warm smile – and produced an excellent lunch. Chagall was very proud of the fact that she was the same age as his daughter Eda, who lived in Paris.

Like so many painters Chagall never had any real sense of value, particularly where his own work was concerned. Years later when I was in the South of France, I invited myself to lunch, and he showed me a dinner service he had recently painted, and which had just been glazed and fired. I knew he was becoming intrigued by ceramics and the plates were exquisite: pale pink, decorated with the delicate Russian folklore motifs that haunt Chagall's work. I wondered who they were for.

'For my daughter,' he explained in his quiet voice. 'When I went into Vence to get her a birthday present, there was nothing worth buying. So I had to make this for her instead.'

The service was priceless, but it is typical of Chagall that he added, almost apologetically, 'I do hope Eda won't be disappointed.'

No doubt Mademoiselle Chagall was delighted when her birthday present arrived, but when Picasso gave a friend of his a wedding gift, it led only to misery.

I had been to see Picasso at Vallauris, finding him for once in an expansive mood, and when I inquired what he had been doing recently, he chuckled, 'Painting somebody's house as a wedding present.'

Picasso had a queer, teasing sense of humour, and perhaps I smiled a little doubtfully, for he added almost angrily, 'Here's the address – go and see for yourself.'

I did, making my way to a narrow slice of an apartment in a block of tall, thin houses in a sunless street. And behind the front door, I found a kaleidoscope of colour.

What had happened was simple. When a young Frenchman called Jean Ramier, who helped Picasso to fire his ceramics, married a local girl, the maestro found them a flat in Vallauris – three rooms, that was all – and then decorated it for them. On the living-room wall he had painted a flowing mural of their wedding procession. The tiny bedroom was decorated with a large nude, the kitchen with the skeleton of a bony fish to represent the lean years, a heaped plate of food for the fat ones. Ramier and his wife paid the landlady the controlled rent of about £2 a week, and the couple settled down to live amidst paintings worth a fortune.

I did not return to Vallauris for three years. Work had taken me to distant places and in truth I had forgotten all about the Ramiers until, staying a long week-end with Somerset Maugham at Cap Ferrat, I was left on my own when Willie lunched out, so drove to Vallauris. The sunless apartment was barred and bolted, but Ramier still worked in the village and, over a Pernod in the Hôtel des Sports, he told me what had happened.

All had gone well, even after the first baby arrived, but when the second was born the Ramiers began to dream of moving to one of the new, ugly modern houses being built on the rim of the village. Yet neither dared voice such thoughts to the other.

The problems increased. The flat was damp. It was difficult to stop the children scratching the walls, and when Madame Ramier tried to clean one painting, she washed away a few square inches of a precious Picasso. Art lovers came in scores to see the tiny flat. An expert from the Louvre even tested the walls, to see if it would be possible to remove the top layer of the plaster, but it was out of the question. Unable to summon up the courage to throw away a fortune by leaving his home, Ramier tried to buy the entire house, with the idea of turning it into a museum, but the bank refused to lend him the money.

It would be pleasant to record that Picasso helped them to resolve their agonising torment, for of course he must have known the dilemma facing the Ramiers. But I imagine (perhaps wrongly) that with his special macabre sense of humour, he was observing the turn of events with a certain relish. Finally Ramier and his wife *did* leave, when they were offered the chance of an ugly prefabricated rabbit hutch. But it had taken them three years to pluck up the courage to throw away a wedding gift which, with supreme irony, was both priceless and valueless.

I soon learned, when interviewing painters for my broad-casts, a cardinal rule: never mention the name of another living painter unless it has been introduced by the subject of the interview. Painters may be generous in spirit but they are quirky, often lonely, and their lives are filled with pet hates and unresolved quarrels. I learned the lesson the hard way. Within weeks of seeing Picasso at Vallauris I went to have lunch with Vlaminck, at his old farmhouse near Veneuil, an hour's drive from Paris.

'What you say is fascinating,' I agreed with something he had just told me. 'As a matter of fact, last month I was talking to Picasso and—'

I thought the roof would fall in. Vlaminck, a picturesque bull of a man with broad shoulders, hands like hams, a pouched, weather-beaten face, roared with hate. 'Don't mention that name in this house! Picasso has dragged French painting into a dead end. There's not a line he draws, not a dab of colour he paints that isn't reminiscent of a document consulted.'

Under the impression that at least some of Picasso's work showed promise, I was about to enter the fray when Madame Vlaminck, like any wife the world over, said soothingly, 'Yes, yes, dear. You are quite right. A horrible man. But let's have lunch.' It took the best part of a bottle of Beaujolais to mollify Vlaminck, for he was a man of violent hates.

Once he drew up a mock will, in which he left to the world all the things he most despised:

To all who wish to accept them, I bequeath the things I don't like, including pasteurised milk, pharmaceutical products, vitamins, all forms of ersatz, and the riddles set by abstract art. For, despite old age, I still like French cooking and the taste of chicken and mushrooms, beefsteak and potatoes, and partridge and cabbage, without confusing cooking with chemistry, the country-side with sanatoria, work with productivity or vice with love.

Lunch with Vlaminck, his wife and two grown-up daughters was never dull. We crowded into a narrow slot of a room next to his study, invariably starting the meal with four or five varieties of home-made *pâté*, usually followed by three chickens – for, as Vlaminck said, chuckling, 'I always like to do things by halves,' meaning, of course, half a chicken each.

After lunch Vlaminck took me to his study, a room with old rafters lining the ceiling, smoke-stained walls, shelves littered with curios – wooden African gods, old paintings, a postcard or two, jars of pickles and jams which Vlaminck had bottled himself, deep, worn leather armchairs, windows looking out over acres of green fields broken only by an occasional 'Vlaminck-style' house or twisted, gnarled tree.

He was in his seventies and his work was deteriorating, for he was turning out pot-boilers. Round the walls hung half a dozen half-finished canvases, all different, all similar. One day after lunch he decided to work and did so – working on seven canvases, using only one colour. For an hour he painted unerring dabs of green where they were needed. Presumably he would add another colour the following day.

Yet at times, he could produce magic with a few deft brush strokes. Once he transformed a pitiful effort of mine merely by adding a non-existent fence in *exactly* the right place, and in *precisely* the right colours.

Why he painted so indifferently in his latter years, I do not know, for he was enormously rich and demanded no luxuries from life. He had never owned a car (perhaps because in his youth he had been a bicycle racer). When his daughters came occasionally to Paris to have supper with me, they had to hire one. 'I despise cars,' he said to me one morning, 'except when I need them.'

But the painter above all others who had no sense of value – or perhaps a *real* sense of value – was the old, frail and adorable Natalie Gontcharova, who lived with her fellow Russian expatriate Michel Larionov in a tiny apartment in the rue de Seine.

These two had had a profound effect on Russian and French art. They had never married, but lived together in two rooms surrounded by hundreds of their paintings which they refused to sell except on a whim, even though they rarely had any ready money.

Canvases and books littered every corner of the rooms. Larionov, a gentle, shambling giant whom I finally drove to the *maison de retraite* where he ended his days, slept on an ancient iron bed which lacked one leg. To prevent the bed sagging under his considerable weight Larionov propped up one corner on books; not dusty, never-to-be-read volumes, but books he consulted regularly, so that if he wanted to check a date or fact for me, I had to hold up the bed (usually littered with canvases) while he withdrew some of the support, substituting another book in its place.

Gontcharova was so gentle and tender, and with such a mischievous smile, that she cried out to be hugged; but I was always afraid that if I did so she might snap. It is hard to describe someone whom one has really loved. The skin on her face was stretched, her hair was wispy and grey, but she had alert, bright eyes: yet to call her a sparrow would be grossly unjust, for she had no perkiness, only the kind of all-embracing love that one would hope for from an old and devoted mother.

She slept, painted, ate, in her tiny room, cluttered with canvases, and if she and Larionov quarrelled (as Russians frequently do) he stayed in the other room while Gontcharova announced with mock severity, 'Today we are divorced.'

I had first met them through the wise and trusted art critic Barnett Conlan, and our friendship grew after Conlan and I helped the two of them to stage a small exhibition in London, where dealers were crying out to display their work. They were, however, too unworldly to face up to the problems of insurance and transport, and did not want to have anything to do with dealers. From time to time I lent them modest sums of money, all of which were repaid from mysterious sources of which I was ignorant; but what I think (and hope) touched them most were our picnic lunches. In summer we drove into the country, perhaps out to the forest of Marly, the car loaded with food cooked by Li; on cold winter days I packed a smaller basket and we enjoyed a *pique-nique* in Gontcharova's room.

I arrived one lunchtime to be met at the top of the rickety stairs by a conspiratorial Larionov who whispered, finger to his lips, 'Gontcharova has a visitor.' He added mysteriously, *'C'est une grande affaire* – a man from the Guggenheim.'

The visitor left shortly, while I was talking in Larionov's room, and we started lunch, the three of us sitting on Gontcharova's bed. The visitor had come from the famous American museum to acquire a Gontcharova for its prestigious collection, and the canvas that had particularly taken his fancy stood in front of the bed – a large square oil, painted in 1908, of some brilliant yellow sunflowers against a background that blazed and lit the room on the cold winter's day.

'I hope you stuck out for a good price?' I said.

'I didn't sell it,' she all but snorted. 'They offered me a lot of money, but they couldn't guarantee that it would be hung for the time being – as though a painting is a sack of coal to be stored in a cupboard.'

We repaired as usual to the Deux Magots for coffee, and I could see that Gontcharova was worried. 'Larionov says we need the money,' she whispered, 'but I refuse to become a coal merchant.' Then after a silence, she added, 'But I'm afraid. The American is coming back tomorrow – and I'm only human. He's very persuasive and I might give in.'

All this was the most casual of conversations, interspersed with greetings to friends and neighbours who popped into the Deux Magots, not only for a coffee, but to get warm behind its steamy windows. We talked of other things too, until without warning Gontcharova clapped her hands with the genuine delight of someone who has solved a difficult problem, and a beautiful smile suffused her face.

'I know what I shall do,' she cried delightedly. 'I know how we can beat the Guggenheim! If I give the painting to Noel, then I can't sell it, can I?'

I am not sure which of us was more astonished as Gontcharova added firmly, 'And no insults about talking money. Call the painting interest on the money you keep lending us.' She added, with one last mischievous smile, 'It's not everyone who is strong enough to beat the museums.'

9

ENTER TITINA

By the early fifties we faced increasing problems with the *Continental Daily Mail*, of which the financial losses were the least worrying; though the annual balance sheet was ablaze with red figures, these could justifiably be absorbed by head office if the *CDM* were regarded as a cheap advertising medium for the London *Daily Mail*. We were in effect handing out fifty thousand 'leaflets' a day, each one bearing the magic words *'Daily Mail'*, in the hope that when readers visited England they would automatically ask for our newspaper. Indeed the name was well known throughout Europe; at a charity football match between French and British teams, one Frenchman who was roughly tackled near my seat by a burly English player jumped up, livid with rage, and spluttered out the only English words he knew: 'Damn and blast! Christmas pudding! *Daily Mail*!'

Our problems went deeper – and were insoluble. In many parts of Europe the *CDM* was being beaten to the bookstalls by the London *Daily Mail*; this was the factor that really caused its closure.

The reason was simple. The French (like the Americans) have no national newspapers. Not only distance, but differing climates and cultures make the people of, say, Marseilles and Paris (or New York and Los Angeles) demand their own newspapers, though the Marseillaise might take a Paris newspaper as well. Britain has a magnificent local press, but here the priorities are reversed: most people take a national newspaper and their local paper as well.

The French system resulted in pitiful distribution outside the Paris area, and even worse in foreign countries. There were no such things as night newspaper planes, as in Britain. In London, with English an international language, British publishers, acting in concert, could guarantee enough freight to encourage BEA to put on night flights. Soon the London *Daily Mail* was on sale in Copenhagen at 11 a.m. – while our newspapers were sitting on the tarmac at Le Bourget until 3 p.m., when the first Paris-Copenhagen flight took off. (In the end I was flying the *CDM* to London to catch the early morning plane to Copenhagen.) Paris itself presented no problems, but we had been proud of our large sales in the South of France – until BEA started night flights to Nice. From that moment the London *Daily Mail* arrived in Nice five hours before the *Continental Daily Mail*.

None of these problems affected our friendly rival, the *New York Herald Tribune*. For even if it arrived 24 hours after the French or British papers, it was still the first American newspaper. The Trib had another advantage; American tourists had money to spend and it easily attracted advertising, whereas we could not, as long as Britain was still rationing foreign currency.

As the life of the paper drew to an end, I also had to undergo the long, dreary – and very sad – rigmarole of a divorce. Helen had finally cried, 'Enough is enough!', and though the proceedings were 'friendly', let no one belittle the agony of splitting up with an old and trusted friend. I was able, of course, to make her an allowance, but in case my pen ran dry, I also cashed the insurance policy which Jack had taken out for me when I was eighteen, and with the money bought Helen the freehold of a flat on the Left Bank. I like to remember that we did remain good friends until she died some years later.

The *Continental Daily Mail* closed in 1953, and the end came not with a whimper but with a bang that could be heard far beyond the rue du Sentier, for we buried her with a wake that lasted until dawn, and only ended when Marie-Lou, in the bistro next door, ran out of plonk.

The death of one's own 'Daily Miracle' is traumatic, for

it cannot be replaced any more than a loved one; but at least when the 'will' was read, every member of the staff was remembered, for Esmond Rothermere insisted on handsome severance pay for those who could not or did not want to be transferred to the London *Daily Mail*.

I now had to consider my own future, for though I was offered a job in London, I was a little apprehensive at the prospect of working for others after running my own show for so many years. Fortunately someone suggested an excellent formula. For a salary and a fixed expense allowance I could go anywhere I liked and airmail a twice-weekly column called 'People on Parade'. The offer was too good to refuse, especially as I had enough contacts around the world to keep me in business.

Among those old friends was Admiral 'Cat' Brown, then Commander of the US Sixth Fleet in the Mediterranean, whom I had met in Paris. I cabled him and within a few days I was accredited to his fleet; so I started my column from his flagship. After that I drove around Europe, looking for subjects, until finally, after a few telephone calls, BOAC offered to fly me to the West Indies, and Edward Molyneux invited me to stay with him at Miranda Hill in Jamaica.

What a life! Edward provided the celebrities, and I wrote about them from my headquarters in a villa that had salt water pumped up to its pool, and even the ultimate luxury of two bathrooms for each double bedroom. ('I can understand people sharing a *bed*, but sharing a *bathroom* is ridiculous,' said the fastidious Edward.)

I might still have been writing my column had my bliss not been shattered by a cable which read:

CAN YOU MAKE SWIFT DIVE BRITISH HON-
DURAS PROIMMEDIATE UPSUMMER POLITI-
CAL SITUATION PARTICULARLY POSITION
COMMUNISTS AND GUATEMALAN INFLU-
ENCE THEREON IN LIGHT COMING ELEC-

TIONS AYE REALLY CONSIDERED SERIOUS
800 WORDS

Where the hell was British Honduras anyway? And *cables*!
I had never sent a press cable in my life (though I had
been issued with cable and airline credit cards in case of
just such an emergency as this). There was nothing for it
but to bid Edward farewell and fly off.

In the plane I did have a niggling feeling that after falling
from a great height in Paris, this unexpected assignment
might offer me the chance to hoist myself back up again,
for I was under no illusion that anyone would miss my
column if I dropped dead. I had nothing to lose, so after
grubbing around in Belize, the capital, for a few hours I
sat down in my hotel bedroom – at forty-three on the brink
of a new and exciting career – and tapped out the first
paragraph of my very first dispatch as a foreign correspondent:

BRITISH HONDURAS IS A BRITISH COLONY
FORGOTTEN BY EVERYONE EXCEPT THE EX-
PORTERS OF GIN . . . .

It made the page 1 splash. Within twenty-four hours I
received a herogram coupled with instructions to proceed
to Guatemala, from which country I cabled two features.
Then another cable summoned me back to Europe to take
a month's leave before being sent to the Far East.

I went to Paris. And it was there that I met Titina.

She was sitting next to me at a luncheon party – a ravishing
dark-haired girl, half Italian, half Romanian. I fell in love
before we had finished the soufflé.

Titina was just over thirty. She had high cheekbones,
an Italian figure (by which I mean that it was not fat but
equally it was not flat) and dark eyes that danced when
she was pleased. We lunched the next day, when she told
me that, like me, she had been married before, but the

marriage had been dissolved ten years previously. She had a son just in his teens, an apartment near the porte de Versailles, and a mother who was visiting her.

We lunched and dined the next day, and the next, and the next, and it seemed that on the whole the course of true love was running smoothly and swiftly, until I discovered I had a rival who very nearly beat me for her hand. This was not a man, but that ogre of international misunderstanding, the US State Department. Titina, it appeared, was in the process of becoming an American citizen, an exercise which demands your physical presence in the United States, to prove that you are not seeking nationality merely for selfish reasons.

'My son will be American too,' she explained in her quaint accent. 'I am alone; I want stability and security – not so much for me, but for him. When I was young, we were all happy in Florence. Then I marry a Frenchman and then we are fighting the Italians. It is too crazy for me – I give up. An American passport is the answer.'

Ten days later – that is, after ten more lunches and dinners – Titina caught the boat train for Cherbourg, and New York. I confess to feeling miserable when she left, but at least I hoped she would be back soon.

The following morning the blow fell. At breakfast there was a letter from her, a sad little note. She hadn't wanted to spoil our happy times together by telling me, but she wasn't returning. The American authorities insisted on at least another year's uninterrupted residence and she was going to look for an apartment in New York.

And then, as I let my coffee grow cold, I couldn't help chuckling at the final paragraph. This was the first of hundreds of letters Titina has written to me, in which time after time she displays the most devastating disregard for the English language. Now, trying to tell me how upset she was, she ended, 'I am very sad. In fact I am not in *équilibre*, and I cannot coagulate my thoughts.'

Neither could I that morning, when Paris suddenly seemed so empty. Then they did 'coagulate' and I swore,

and cut myself shaving when I realised what a fool I was
to let this delicious creature slip out of my life.

I am often accused of being impulsive, but I have never
been quite so impulsive before or since. I found out when
her ship docked and booked a tourist flight to New York,
timed to arrive the night before she did. I also booked a
return flight for two for the following night.

At eight o'clock that morning, I was on the pier in New
York to meet her. She seemed a trifle surprised, but telling
her to leave her heavy luggage in bond – 'It'll be sent back
to Paris soon,' I informed her airily – I whisked her away
to the St Regis, gave her a large Gibson, and started, as
lucidly as I could, to explain the enormous advantages of
possessing a British passport, in addition of course to a
British husband.

I had already planned to use part of my leave to research
an article in Rome for the *Saturday Evening Post*; on the
flight back to Paris I suggested she should join me on
the Italian assignment, to make sure our vital statistics
matched.

10

LADIES FIRST

MARRIAGE AT ANY time is a risky business, but the prospect of remarriage is positively daunting, and I was terrified. Almost at once I had to face up to my first sacrifice – no, not my independence, far worse: my devoted and irreplaceable Li.

For eight years Li and I had had a perfect understanding. He preferred a male household, though if some lady (who had perhaps fallen asleep) remained on a temporary basis after sampling Li's excellent cooking, he clucked conspiratorially. However, the least sign of a more permanent liaison produced sulks and a consequent deterioration in the quality of the cuisine.

Titina and I had spent two weeks driving back from Rome, helped no doubt by the glorious weather and a belief I share fervently with Leigh Hunt:

The two divinest things this world has got,
A lovely woman in a rural spot.

Once back in the rue des Saints-Pères, it seemed foolish for Titina to risk the night air and return to her apartment, and the next morning Li served her breakfast with a beatific smile, basking in the reflected prowess [*sic*] of his master; and when I returned home that evening, Titina having gone, Li beamed at me and said, 'Madame is very beautiful, sir.'

'I think so too,' I said, adding almost without thinking, 'In fact, we're going to get married.'

His face seemed to crumple. And then, at the prospect of a woman ruining our perfect *ménage*, a single tear welled in the corner of his eye and rolled down his crinkled, parchment cheek. I had known the man for years but had not imagined that he had feelings deeper than normal loyalty.

The next morning Li did not turn up. I tried in vain to find him, but he had left the address he had given me some months previously and I never saw him again.

That week I received a letter from my friend Admiral 'Cat' Brown of the US Sixth Fleet, to whom I had written to tell him about Titina. Remembering no doubt my abject fear when being lowered by winch from a helicopter on to a destroyer, he wrote:

> The courage of Noel Baker is legendery [*sic*] but Goda-mighty, there is something that defeats understanding and makes strong men grow pale and falter in the tale you unfold. Is it a form of deathless courage or sheer madness that causes a man in middle age in a well-ordered life, to suddenly take the plunge.
>
> Yours in awed curiosity,
> CAT BROWN

Though I have by now been a happily married man (whatever that really means) for many years, I never cease to be amazed at the hidden warnings that lie behind the happy smiles of the married couples I know. The apartment in Paris where I first met Titina was the scene of an apparently successful and well-ordered *mariage de convenance* that cloaked more ironic twists than a Maugham short story.

I had become a friend of Sir Charles Mendl, who lived in some style in the avenue d'Iéna, when I first arrived in Paris. He gave a daily luncheon for a dozen or so people (always starting with a cheese soufflé) at which one could be certain to meet the finest selection of pretty girls in the French capital. (That is why Titina was there.)

Charles, who was born in 1871, had been Press Attaché at the British Embassy until 1940; his first wife, the famous Hollywood interior decorator Elsie Wolf, had died. By the time I knew him he looked his age. Because illness prevented him from taking exercise he was, as he put it, 'well padded'. His hair was thin, but his cheeks were still chubby, and nothing could erase his smile. He played the part of a man who had lived well, loved well, and was determined to enjoy what life was left to him.

He did. At the age of eighty, Charles married again, a truly enchanting red-headed divorcée called Yvonne Riley, whom he had known some years previously in America, after which their ways had parted. After Elsie Mendl died, they came together again, Charles an old man, rich but often in a wheelchair, she young, beautiful – and penniless. Marriage had not at first been discussed, but Charles, who had no children, decided to leave Yvonne his fortune. Not so simple in France, where the inheritance laws are among the few that cannot be broken, and where distant cousins outrank closest friends when the will comes to be read.

There was only one way out, and Charles took it. He married Yvonne. Everyone adored her, and she became a solicitous wife to an old man who had loved her and was thanking her in the nicest possible way. If she bestowed any favours on others they were given with the utmost discretion. But most of all, she transformed his apartment into a centre of youth and beauty, running it from her huge bathroom-cum-boudoir with its white carpet, record player and watchful white cat, Rachmaninoff.

It was hardly a bed and butter marriage, but since Charles was very old it might have had a happy ending, leaving Yvonne a beautiful and rich young widow, had not two things happened. Yvonne fell in love. This in itself was not tragic, for all she had to do was remain discreet – and wait. But then she was stricken with cancer of the most virulent kind, and the doctors gave her only a few months to live. And so, ironically, she missed out on life on all counts.

I must say, she never lost her sense of humour. When I saw her shortly before her death, she managed to chuckle,

'If I pull through this illness, I'm going to sue Charles for breach of contract.'

Married life is full of pitfalls, as a very different but equally exciting Paris hostess discovered. Rosita Winston, older than poor Yvonne, was a striking black-haired American, with a touch of Cherokee Indian, who had acquired an imposing residence (really, the word 'house' is not enough) in the rue St-Dominique, where she entertained lavishly while Norman, her agreeable but self-effacing husband, worked hard in New York's real-estate jungle, finally owning a chunk of Broadway before his premature death. (It reminded me of the chestnut in which an American wife gushes, 'My husband and I both *adore* Paris, and when one of us dies, I'm going to live there.')

Norman was alive in those days, and I have not seen Rosita for many years, but she was a darling. A snob, yes, but open-hearted, vivacious, imperious when dressed to the eyes by 'darling Jacques' (Fath) or 'dearest Edward' (Molyneux).

In common with many rich American hostesses, Rosita liked to indulge herself in the luxury of collecting a few titled acquaintances for her parties. She was not a woman to do things by halves, and when she collected a beautiful lioness, with a title to fit, she invited her for Christmas, and gave her $1,000 mad money to spend on Fifth Avenue.

I was in New York at the time and heard the story at first hand. All went well until Rosita mixed up her date with the hairdresser and on arrival there found him closed. Meanwhile Norman, who had been casting longing eyes at the foreign contessa, and apprised of his wife's rendezvous with the crimper, rushed back from Wall Street and made straight for the lady's room. His amorous advances were not, it seems, rebuffed, for according to Rosita, when she returned Norman had already pressed his suit to the point of having taken off his trousers.

After kicking Norman out of the house (for the time being) Rosita locked the contessa in her room and left her there until the butler had acquired a reservation for her on

the next train to California. It was left to the New York
columnist Cholly Knickerbocker to sum up the misadventure with the classic sentence, 'Mrs Winston returned home
unexpectedly to find Mr Winston overentertaining the
guest.'

Rosita was not the only American woman I knew with a
tempestuous temperament. I once spent three months in
Mexico with another American, Dorothy di Frasso, who
was very rich – she had inherited $12 million and owned
half of Lord and Taylor's in New York – and had married
into a noble Italian family, though when I met her in 1945,
during a break in my mission to America, she was living
alone in Acapulco.

I had arrived in what was then a charming little resort
with no money, but an ardent desire to stay as long as
possible and enjoy the sun and big game fishing. Fortunately an old friend, Camille Cianfarra of *The New York
Times* (later drowned in the *Andrea Doria*), introduced
me to Dorothy. With a typical American wave of the hand,
she said, 'Stay as long as you like!'

She was restless, almost birdlike, never still, always
riffling her hands through her hair, smoking incessantly
through a cigarette holder. My stay was helpful to both of
us because Dorothy needed companionship, someone to
talk to and play gin with – nothing more, for though her
heart did not belong to the dashing Count di Frasso, she
had bequeathed it to a shabby little crook called Bugsy
Siegel, one of the heads of 'Murder Incorporated'. Happily
for my peace of mind he was at that time in California.
Bugsy was no ordinary gangster. A rapist and murderer
before he was twenty-one, he was handsome, dashing and
enjoyed socialising (between murders). Dorothy had taken
him up – even inviting him before the war to her sumptuous palazzo the Villa Madama in Rome.

She was infatuated, and violently jealous. She was becoming increasingly incensed at rumours that Bugsy had
fallen for a Hollywood actress called Virginia Hill, younger

and more well-favoured than Dorothy. Indeed one newspaper described her as 'The Best Lay on the West Coast', so poor Dorothy had no chance. At breakfast one morning on the balcony at Acapulco the previous day's English-language newspaper arrived as we were scooping out papaw sprinkled with fresh lime juice. On the front page was the stark announcement that Bugsy had moved into Miss Hill's apartment in Beverly Hills.

'The shit!' The Countess never forgot she was American-born, and had a remarkable command of the vernacular. 'The bloody sod!' With that she did the only thing her turbulent character would allow. Still in her flimsy négligé, all frills and coloured ribbon and little else, she tore out to the imposing front drive, jumped into the nearest car – it happened to be a brand-new Cadillac – and drove it as fast as she could into the nearest tree.

Dorothy did not kill herself, only vented her wrath; anyway Bugsy was later shot between the eyes by rival mobsters. Nor did Dorothy die of a broken heart, but she nearly broke mine, for the Cadillac had been earmarked for my personal use until the time came for me to leave.

If the chequered lives of my friends were anything to go by, the outlook was gloomy as I contemplated taking the step which Saki ruefully described as 'the western custom of one wife and hardly any mistresses' – an observation not to be taken lightly, for if it is true that a man finds it impossible to remain faithful to the woman he loves, it is equally true that he is almost always found out.

Perhaps Clark Gable's advice was the best. The last time I met Clark was in Paris, where he said to me, 'Women will give you everything they have – so long as you don't marry 'em. But once you sign on the dotted line, they think it's a ration card.'

True or false? I only need think of another friend who tried both alternatives with zeal and passion for years, and failed with both the woman who became his wife, and with the one who became his long-standing mistress. The man was Aly Khan and, as it happened, I knew both girls. The wife was Rita Hayworth, whom I met several times, and the girl was Gene Tierney, the actress, who happens to be Titina's cousin.

Aly *was* a good friend, generous and kind, a wonderful host with impeccable manners. I met him first through his father, the old Aga Khan. I was never a bosom friend, but we did go dancing from time to time with a couple of girls, and I was able to observe his extraordinary ability to make a woman firmly believe that no other woman in the world existed for him. There was no trick in the way he made them swoon. I have seen the eyelids flutter on grandmothers who danced with him, for at that moment, that woman was the only one Aly thought about.

It was Aly who introduced me to Rita. Shortly after their wedding in the South of France, Aly gave a huge reception at the Ritz in Paris, and as it broke up, Elsa Maxwell insisted on driving with Aly back to his house in the Bois. 'Be an angel and drive Rita home, will you?' Aly asked me. This is why I spent half an hour in the back of the office car with one of the most beautiful women in the world.

I liked her then, and even more when we met again. She was 'one of us' – by which I mean that she was a working girl who had started at six as a dancer, had become a movie star but had not allowed herself any traces of snootiness. Yet almost from the start, her marriage to Aly was doomed – because of the way Aly treated her, the way he could not *help* but treat her, because of deep instincts beyond his control.

Aly was a Moslem, not only by belief and as a leader of the Ismaili sect, but in character, in race, in every drop of blood that coursed so eagerly through his veins. Deep down in his subconscious, below the façade of western charm he presented to the world, he regarded himself as an Oriental prince to whom the thought of sharing a woman was abhorrent. So it is to me, but 'sharing a woman' has a very different connotation in the East. To us, sharing a wife usually means in a horizontal position. In the East it means sharing her beauty, which should be for the eyes of one beholder only. Hence the harem and the veil.

Rita was shown off on special occasions much as a precious jewel is displayed by a proud owner, but never out of the owner's sight. Barely a month after we met, Aly gave his annual dinner dance at the Pré Catelan in the Bois de Boulogne, the most glittering evening of the Paris summer social season. I noticed then (and on subsequent occasions) that Aly danced every dance, each time with a different partner. Rita never danced once. She stood there, smiling and beautiful, but she never danced. I imagine she had been forbidden to.

A few months later I saw her again, as I was finishing a boisterous lunch in a bistro with Sam White, the Paris columnist. By three o'clock we were the only customers left in the restaurant. Aly and Rita walked in, hoping, I am sure, that the restaurant would be empty. As Aly waved to me, I was shocked at Rita's appearance. She wore no make-up, her hair was tousled, she looked tired, even ill.

The truth is that Aly did not like his women to be the subject of envious glances from other men. *He* knew how beautiful she was. There was no need to display it in public any more than one would unveil a woman of the harem in public. Elsa Maxwell told me once that Rita had the greatest difficulty in persuading Aly to let her go to a hairdresser or beauty parlour.

Rita walked out on Aly, and soon Titina's cousin, the glamorous Gene Tierney, entered the scene. Two years younger than Rita, Gene, with her exquisitely chiselled face, was a New York socialite who had turned to the stage and then films, making (among many others) the splendid *Laura*. She, like Rita, never danced at the annual ball, and finally she and Aly split.

Gene, however, was not built of such tough fibre as Rita. After returning to America she had a mental break-down that lasted for several years until friends finally brought her out of the dark world to reality and got her a job – as a salesgirl in a shop. Because Gene is loved by all who know her, everyone tried to help. Otto Preminger, the film producer, gave her parts in several films, and now she is happily married – and saved.

So Aly lost out. Though theoretically a great success with women, his attitude to them almost always led to disaster. Nothing lasted. Inevitably he started searching desperately for the right woman. And the only way was to try as many as possible. (He certainly had the staying power for this exercise.) It was this that branded him with the public image of 'the great lover', and this image finally took over his much more modest personality, forcing him to live up to it. This in turn made the old Aga pass over Aly as his successor. It was a tragedy, for Aly was highly admired by his followers, and would have made a much loved Aga Khan.

11

AND SO TO WED

ACCORDING TO THE heavenly bodies our marriage should long ago have ended in divorce. There had already been warning signs of incompatibility. For the first week or two after our wedding we camped out in my Paris apartment, while Titina's mother and son stayed on in hers.

Arriving home on the Left Bank one evening I saw a knot of people curiously regarding an unusual object on the pavement. It was a large mattress for a double bed. It was *my* large mattress, and it had obviously been thrown out of the window. My first thought, as a law-abiding citizen, was to send for the *flics* – until, having gone upstairs, a triumphant Titina kissed me, led me to the bedroom, displayed a new mattress, produced the bill, and announced, 'I know what's been going on here. Now at last this apartment is *clean*.'

'But you can't just throw money out of the window like that,' I protested. 'And anyway, you had no complaints when we used the bed before we got married.'

'Ah! That was different,' explained Titina. 'I would have slept in *any* bed, I was so tired after all those fields you insisted on stopping in during the drive to Paris.'

This sort of problem I could handle easily. A tickle here, an odd slap there, soon put differences like this into perspective. I did, however, face the more intractable foe of the stars. Titina was an ardent disciple of the experts who cast horoscopes and insist that ill-matched couples can often trace their divorces to the fact that they were born under differing signs precluding all possibility of harmony.

'I'm not stupid about it, but I do believe in the stars,'

101

said Titina. 'An expert told me that my marriage to Gaby [her first husband] was bound to fail because our birthdays were anti-happy. Perhaps that's why you and Helen divorced.'

We newly married men have other things to think about (such as money and mattresses) than the idle prattling of a beautiful woman. 'Could be,' I said, reaching for the whisky.

'By the way, when's your birthday?' she asked. 'Is it soon – do I have to start saving up for a present?'

'Not long to wait,' I replied. 'It's the ninth of September.'

If this were a novel I could assert that Titina turned pale; though it was too dark for me to see, I am sure she did. She was very quiet for a moment before announcing in a small voice, 'It's not possible! Gaby was born on the ninth of September.'

'Forget it!' I tried to cheer her up. 'Come to that, when do I have to start saving for *your* birthday?'

'It's not until the sixteenth of December.'

I put my glass of Scotch down with such a bang that the whisky slopped over the table. It was my turn to be silent, and I am sure that I paled.

'How very odd,' I said finally. 'Helen was also born on the sixteenth of December.'

What I like about the Italians is their resilience. The double coincidence was so incredible that a normal woman would have moped for weeks. Not Titina.

'We will beat the stars,' she cried, 'but to do that we must leave this sordid apartment and start afresh. Let's go and live in Switzerland.'

We did just that. On our marathon journey from Rome to Paris we had stayed a couple of nights at Rolle, a delightful small town midway between Geneva and Lausanne. The lake lies gently in front of the main street, with snow on the mountains that dominate it; behind the vineyards sweep up to the skyline.

I now took a week's holiday and drove back to Rolle in my old but spanking Citroën. Once installed in the Domino

Hotel at Rolle, we discovered that the local estate agent was a Monsieur Peter who was also mayor, bank manager, even head of the water board.

It was Sunday evening, and Monsieur Peter's various establishments were not open. Unfortunately the antique shop opposite Domino was. We repaired there to take a look round, and the first thing Titina saw was a truly beautiful, large fireplace. 'I can see the log fire burning inside it,' she whispered.

'Don't be silly,' I whispered back. 'One of the first things you need for a fireplace is a house.'

'I'll buy it for your birthday,' cried Titina suddenly, and it was, I have to admit, the only time anyone has bought me a fireplace for a birthday.

In her singsong Vaudois accent the antique dealer asked where she should deliver our purchase.

I stumbled, audibly.

'Actually,' said Titina sweetly, 'we haven't got a house yet. Would you mind keeping it until we find one?'

The woman choked, muttered something about '*les anglais*', and we marched out, heads high.

The next morning, on the way to see Monsieur Peter, I warned Titina, 'Now, buying property is a very serious business. We've got to be careful. We'll comb the lakeside and look at every single empty dwelling before deciding anything.'

We bought the damn house before lunch. It was the only one we ever looked at. It was at the end of a country lane, with a high hedge, a dozen fruit trees, a fair slice of land, and in front of the kitchen and barn doors a fountain that spilled water into a trough where once the horses had drunk. The house was long and low and built of stone.

'Amusing,' I said nonchalantly to Monsieur Peter, a dignified gentleman, as befits a lord high everything. The house had no water laid on, no drains, no heating, no lighting. But it was a house that no one could fail to love.

The trouble was that all I possessed in the world was about £2,000 and a few paintings. We repaired to Monsieur

Peter's bank, where I explained my predicament. I would like to own the house, but I had no money, usually regarded as an insuperable obstacle to the acquisition of material objects.

'My dear sir' – Monsieur Peter gave me a benign smile – 'money is the *least* of our worries.' Whereupon the gallant mayor introduced us to a quaint Swiss banking custom I strongly urge other countries to emulate. 'May we continue this discussion over a bottle of wine?' he suggested.

With a touch of ceremony he opened a stout door at the rear of his office, through which we walked down into a wine cellar, gravel on the floor, hundreds of bottles lining the walls. He uncorked a bottle of good Swiss wine and we toasted our new home. With the possibility of future overdrafts I opened an account with Monsieur Peter on the spot, after buying the house for £1,000 down – keeping the rest for contingencies.

When my hesitant mention of the word 'references' had been waved away with a polite, 'But Monsieur Barber, you are *English*,' Monsieur Peter made arrangements for his friends the decorators, electricians, carpenters, to give us all the credit we needed. He even found a bungalow where Titina, her mother and Musty, her son by her previous marriage, could live while superintending the house repairs.

I had to leave soon afterwards, for Korea, as it happened, followed by trips all over the world. Sometimes I was away for three or four months at a time. Titina of course needed a car to get around the countryside, so I left her my Citroën, pride and joy of my life. It shows the depth of my love that she was the first woman who ever drove it. There seemed to be no problem, after she told me she had an Italian licence.

Alas, I did not then know the ways of Italy, nor that in that heavenly country people with a pull roar with laughter at the idea of such silly things as taking driving tests. If you have the right contacts you get a licence and *then* you have a shot at driving. When I left Titina at Geneva airport and casually showed her the gear positions, I thought she looked a trifle startled, but put it down to wifely sorrow at our parting.

Those first three months in the Far East seemed like a year, but at least I had a new hobby – deciphering Titina's letters. She wrote regularly, but Titina is as impatient as she is beautiful, and though she actually speaks very good English, she tends to make up words if she does not have the correct ones to hand. She says it is quicker than searching for a dictionary, a point which had not hitherto occurred to me; and of course until our marriage she had spoken but never written our tongue.

When I was in climates cold, a letter implored me, 'Please, darling, be careful not to catch ammonia.' When I forgot to reply to specific questions about the house, I was reproved, 'You must please reed my letters more attentiously.' Then she had 'a sore froat and can hardly brief'. At least she received letters from me regularly, 'and you will never know how eech lettre is a frill'. The repairs to the house were expensive, but she tried to keep down the cost, telling me so with, 'I can promise you deer, I will never be spendencious.' There was a minor crisis when her mother hurt her hand: 'She put it in mistake in scaldacious water, but despite our disordinate life, we are happy.'

Finally I arrived home at Geneva airport – yes, 'home' – and looked in blank dismay at the tattered remains of my fastest girl friend, the Citroën. Somehow Titina had managed not only to dent almost every part of the body, but even to knock numbers off the licence plates.

'Now listen, dammit—' I began.

'Yes, darling,' said Titina nervously. 'I do listen. I suspend your lips.' Which is why there never was a row about the Citroën. What the hell's a car anyway?

When we married I imagined that even if two could not live as cheaply as one, two could live as cheaply as two. Ah me, the innocence of us simple Yorkshire folk. Within

two years our farmhouse in Switzerland was inhabited
by nine people, and there were almost nine languages
stuttering from room to room like a recording session at
an examination for interpreters. Admittedly I was away
a great deal, and Titina managed magnificently, but to
understand each other we seemed to have to speak English,
French, Italian, Danish, German, with a little Romanian
and Korean thrown in for good measure.

There was the breadwinner, the only Englishman in the
house. There was Titina, to whom I spoke usually in
French or English. I now had a son Bengy, eighteen
months old, who was starting to speak in French or Italian,
and Simonetta, who was still silent. There were two other
children. Musty, Titina's son, was sixteen and as French
as they come. Fine, I could cope easily. But then Titina
adopted her niece whom she had brought up during World
War Two, a ravishing seventeen-year-old called Manuela.
She spoke only Italian. We needed help in the house, and
Swiss help cost the earth, so before Simonetta arrived I
arranged for a friend in Denmark to send us a Danish au
pair. She spoke only Danish, plus enough basic English to
allow her and Titina to prevent the children from starving
to death.

That accounted for seven. But we faced another problem: how could we organise life so that occasionally Titina
could come away with me on a trip? Being old-fashioned,
she flatly refused to leave the children unless we asked
Titina's mother to come and live with us. This was Mamie,
a remarkable Romanian lady of seventy-one whose best
languages were unfortunately Romanian and Korean, the
latter language having been learned when her late husband
was Ambassador in Seoul. Finally there was Else, our
treasure, who came from a small village near Zug and
spoke only Swiss German, a language not to be tolerated
unless one is discussing numbered accounts.

Of course all this took money, and luckily for me, I
seemed to be able to keep pace. On the strictly practical
side, I had, during a month's newspaper strike in 1955,

occupied my time by taking a crash course in the rudiments of television production, and soon I managed to get a contract to make twenty-six half-hour documentaries for ARTV, to go out fortnightly under the general title 'Assignment Unknown'. The idea behind the series was simple. I would go wherever the *Daily Mail* sent me – and they sent me just about everywhere in those days. Between filing stories, I would find subjects that made good, short TV documentaries. Their subjects varied widely; one was about a group of British WVS girls left behind in Korea, another about a missionary in a leper colony in Africa. This way the television company saved a fortune in expenses and the *Daily Mail* gained the publicity of having one of its foreign correspondents appearing regularly on TV. It was bloody hard work, but I needed the money – though I nearly didn't get it all. On the flight to London to sign the contract I was talking about it to a lawyer friend who happened to be on the plane.

'For heaven's sake,' he gasped. 'If you sign in England you could be liable to British tax.'

I took the next plane back, and a grateful TV executive, armed with a ball-point pen, came to spend the week-end with us in Rolle.

In those days – the late fifties – life in Switzerland was nothing like as expensive as it is today, especially with the low rates of income tax prevailing. We were further helped by our redoubtable friend Monsieur Peter, who could always be relied upon to assist us when necessary – as for example when the water supply was laid on at the farm.

We had never received a real estimate from the Rolle Corporation, and when the bill arrived I was horrified. At the time we bought the house I had asked Peter whether it would be expensive, and he had given me a rough estimate which I had accepted in good faith; this bill was double what I had been told.

'Oh hell,' I sighed to Titina. 'I suppose there's nothing one can do about it.'

'Isn't there?' Titina almost snorted. 'Have you never

heard about mistakes being made? Let's go and see Monsieur Peter.'

How right she was – and how little I knew about the all-embracing powers of the genial mayor of Rolle.

'But of course,' said Monsieur Peter, 'there must be an error. I will write to the councillor in charge of the water board immediately.'

I still have copies of the correspondence. The first letter, addressed to the chairman of the water board, complained of the error, and it was signed, 'Henri Peter, Mayor'.

The reply, which was addressed formally to the Mayor, admitted and regretted the mistake, and was signed 'Henri Peter, Water Department'.

Life was not all roses for the head of a polyglot family. Once when I returned, the Danish au pair was on the point of leaving. Being half Danish, I could understand the reason she gave: she was pining for a good Danish *smörgåsbord*. I solved that one by telephoning cousin Gitte in Copenhagen – by now happily married – and she arranged to air-freight a complete Danish meal to Geneva airport. That kept the girl quiet for a while.

In the end she did leave, and there was nothing for it but to replace her with a Swiss girl, especially as we needed a trained nanny for Simonetta. The girl came to us with impeccable references, a silver badge of office on a chain round her neck, an inordinate quantity of stiffly starched clothes, and I must say she kept Simmy quiet and happy. Simmy was a darling and thank God she slept – anything up to twenty hours a day in those first few weeks, which meant that whenever she woke up she was in a happy temper and wonderful to play with.

Simmy might still have been asleep had Titina not become puzzled by the way she seemed to be losing the modest family silver: small items like sugar tongs, silver salt cellars, an occasional silver-plated salver. Titina is normally so watchful that I began to wonder what had happened to her.

I was enjoying a quiet cigar in the garden one day when Titina called me urgently. 'Come – be quick – I've got something to show you.'

She led me into Simmy's room, in which the nanny slept. 'It's her day off, and I've been searching her room,' she said.

Under a pile of starched linen were all our silver trifles, each one wrapped up in preparation for the approaching Christmas, each one labelled as gifts for friends.

That was bad enough. 'But look at this,' said Titina.

'This' was in another drawer – nearly a score of books on do-it-yourself sex, with every position clearly illustrated, while other books contained dialogues from blue movies, a third erotic poetry.

That was bad enough. 'But look at *this*,' said Titina.

'This' was the most terrible thing of all. Tucked away in a corner of a drawer was an envelope which no one would have thought of opening – except Titina. It contained a dozen or so sleeping tablets, each one carefully broken into small pieces, to be used at the first infant squeal.

No wonder we called Simmy the sleeping beauty.

No, life was not all roses for a polyglot papa. I liked to know where every one of my lovingly collected books was; they tended to be borrowed. I liked to wipe each classical record with one of those anti-dust cloths; it seemed to vanish every time I wanted to play a little Mozart. What a damned nuisance four children of different ages can be when one has acquired them in a matter of two or three years. The teenagers whom I had never watched growing and who came to me off the peg, so to speak, could be insufferable. Musty pined for Paris. Manuela fell in love – regularly, and with the wrong men. And fancy having a maid who could talk only German. No, there was a tough side to the life of a polyglot papa. And then suddenly everything clicked. I shall always remember the moment.

I arrived back at Geneva's homely airport at 5 a.m. after a rough time in the Congo. I joined the crocodile of people filing towards the immigration and customs, and I thought, sleepily, 'Well, here it goes again, the worst part of my job, landing lonely with the dawn.' I would get a taxi for the half-hour journey to the farm; but how I hated those lonely landings.

I walked through the customs shed, cleared my battered old suitcase – and there they were, the whole family, screaming and yelling. They had driven into Geneva to meet me. Bengy hit a policeman as he recognised me – I swear he did – and cried, ' 'Allo, papa!' Manuela and Titina planted kisses on my cheeks. Musty, too grown up for this sort of nonsense, asked with the gravest urgency – in French, of course – if I felt like a game of tennis after breakfast.

We all drove home singing in the car. The flowers were out, the apples were ripening. Mamie welcomed me in Romanian – or was it Korean?

I went to my room to change after taking a bath. A huge pile of bills was waiting for me; but what the hell, it was only money. All over the house a babel of tongues was working overtime, all planning life for polyglot papa. I was home – that's all there was to it, I was home.

12

DERRING-DO DATELINE

THE DERRING-DO DATELINE is all things to all men, especially
married men. What bliss for a happily married man to
return home after a profitable trip abroad and sink into
the arms of his loved ones without the prospect of any
immediate work. And what bliss for an unhappily married
man to be *ordered* to leave a nagging wife and irksome
children for months on end.

I loved the life of the headline hunter. True, it is always
supposed to be spiced with danger, but in fact I seldom
heard a shot fired in anger (though in Budapest a rotter
did take a pot shot at me). For the most part I roamed the
world at someone else's expense, more often than not to
places I would never otherwise have seen. I have sat on
the creaking wooden veranda of the only hotel at Ujiji at
the very spot where Stanley met Livingstone. I have sat in
front of a broad, sluggish yellow river, the bank lined with
Malayan houses on piles, drinking a sundowner with a
rubber planter. I have landed at Muscat, capital of Oman,
and been handed, most gravely, a bicycle lamp to carry
when walking the streets at night. One day in Harbin, a
local Manchurian took me to the golf course, which had a
sign prominently displayed, 'No golfers allowed on the
course without revolvers'.

I had many splendid colleagues but none more agreeable
than Donald Wise, ex-parachutist, ex-rubber planter, and
by the time I met him, roving correspondent for the *Daily
Express*. Well over six feet tall, he always wore trousers
so tight he seemed to have been poured into them; he
sported a brief aggressive moustache – the sort he could
twitch by moving the corner of his mouth. A passionate

sun-worshipper, he was always tanned, always by the nearest pool when not filing.

There was no pool when we travelled together from Khartoum to Kosti, a hundred and fifty miles or so south of the Sudanese capital, where there had been yet another example of the lack of feeling, care, even basic intelligence, that so often stigmatises the police forces in newly 'liberated' African dictatorships.

The northern Sudanese hold no brief for any tribes living south of the capital anyway, and when the locals at Kosti staged a mass rally the police bundled four hundred demonstrators into a large warehouse, forgetting to open the windows which were out of reach of the prisoners. Three hundred died, an outrage which the Sudanese government tried to hush up, thinking in their innocence that if they cancelled all rail and bus services to a township that had no airfield, it would deter any inquisitive journalists. Donald and I took a taxi, agreeing to split the fare which came to £160.

We reached Kosti, cabled our despatches, then looked around for something that would give us an extra story in the vicinity (on the principle that newspaper accountants tend to relate unusually high expenses to the number of words produced). An Englishman from one of the meat packing firms in the area told us that an agricultural development school had opened not far away, and our eager driver pointed his ancient Buick in what he hoped was the right direction.

The area was dotted with Masai villages, the homes of tall, graceful men and women who paint themselves all over, wear little clothing, and live largely on a mixture of blood and milk – the blood being extracted with spears once a week from the necks of long-suffering cattle whose wounds are healed by mud poultices before the milk is extracted at the other end.

We lost our way. The driver spoke little English, and drove happily along, one cheery eye on the meter, and we were about to turn back when we saw a Masai on the outskirts of a small village. He was naked except for a shawl thrown over his shoulders, and his tall thin frame, which rested languidly on a long spear, was painted ochre.

'Leave this to me,' said Don. Jumping out of the car, he prepared to use the expertise he had accumulated when handling rubber tappers in Malaya.

'Hey, you tall fellow,' he began affably, as befits a white man in a black country, 'you hear tell of big new school to make plants grow big like you? Like the story of Jack and beanstalk?'

'Good morning, old man,' drawled the naked Masai, still leaning on his spear. 'You mean our agricultural school? A showpiece, old boy, I can tell you. Right through the village and three miles along the road.'

As we gaped, he added. 'I say – are you newspaper chaps? Oh, *well*! I met a lot of you blokes when I was at Cambridge. I'll take you there!'

We were lucky. Our naked friend had studied for three years at Cambridge, taken his degree in agriculture, and thought it perfectly natural to take off all his clothes the moment he returned to the village of which he was chief.

I hope all is well with Donald Wise, but I am worried, for some time ago I heard a rumour that he had inherited a quarter of a million pounds – just the kind of bad luck that can ruin a good man's career.

There was no end to the derring-do datelines. I once landed by ski-plane on an iceberg in the Arctic Ocean to report on the work of scientists voluntarily 'marooned' near the North Pole; and no sooner had I completed the mission and returned to Fairbanks, than I was ordered to fly from freezing Alaska to tropical Guam on another story. I did not even have time to collect my laundry, but then people all over the world have inherited my dirty washing, left when ordered to move at a moment's notice.

Speed was the name of the game. Once when hard news was scarce, someone suggested that I try to fly round the world by commercial airlines (in those pre-jet days) in eighty hours to coincide with the release of the film *Around the World in Eighty Days*. Because of the differing time zones, the hours I spent aloft were divided into five nights and three days. I was robbed of one day of my life and it has never been returned to me.

It was all good clean fun, rather like a continuing series from the *BOP* or *Chums*, with no holds barred, as when, in the true spirit of the derring-do dateline, Donald Wise once chased me to India – despite the fact that I was on my way to Greenland. Before I departed on a big 'set-piece' story, the *Mail* announced, 'Barber has left for – where?', probably adding, 'Watch this space.' Someone on the *Express* discovered details of the flight on which a Barber was booked to India, and Wise was deputed to chase me – only to find himself in the next seat to Stephen Barber of the *Daily Telegraph*.

The main danger when racing round the world and filing within hours of reaching a trouble spot lay in checking facts in time to reach a deadline. Most of us (and that certainly includes me) have sinned when obeying the injunction of one well-known Fleet Street foreign editor who invariably snarled to raw recruits, 'If you wanna succeed, never check an exciting fact.' For 'facts,' as Somerset Maugham wrote, 'are often very tiresome'; and the temptation not to confirm them could result in waspish cables from head office. None was more succinct than that which reached Arthur Cook. Arthur was the delightful and hard-working foreign correspondent who, during the expropriation of Anglo-Iranian Oil in 1951, heard from 'an unimpeachable source' that the Iranian premier, the hated Mossadegh, had been assassinated. It was exclusive; it led his paper. Unhappily Mossadegh proved the report premature, at which Arthur received an historic cable from his foreign editor: 'EITHER YOU OR MOSSADEGH DIES TONIGHT.'

Headlines are a popular newspaper's simplest method of attracting a reader's immediate attention. Sometimes, however, the name of one man in a headline would encourage people to read about a different man in the story. This was why brother Tony and I became involved in a couple of 'inverted' headlines when both of us were in the news.

Tony, who was MP for Doncaster, was appointed Parliamentary Private Secretary to Harold Macmillan, then prime minister. I was stabbed in Casablanca, at a time when several Frenchman a day were being killed.

My brush with the Arabs took place just before midnight as I was making my way back to the Hôtel El Mansour after filing a cable. There was a short-cut between the well-lit boulevard des Quatre Zouaves and the hotel, hardly more than two hundred yards long, and as I turned into it someone pounced on my back, presumably thinking I was French and therefore fair game.

I don't wish to be heroic about what was after all only the Casablanca equivalent of a mugging, but the man, who was dressed in a burnous, had a very large knife and kept hacking away from the back. I was hampered in defending myself because of his flowing robes. Suddenly – maybe everything happened in thirty seconds – I realised he was going to kill me. Just in time I remembered an RAF commando trick, and managed to get one hand near his face, and then plucked out an eye. At which he loosed his grip and I bolted, or rather crawled, back to the hotel.

As far as I was concerned, the *Daily Mail* made great play of this incident in which their heroic [*sic*] reporter had been knifed five times by an Arab, and as I had started my newspaper career in Doncaster, where Jack was still chairman of the magistrates' bench, the local paper felt that this should be reported. But who the hell would remember a junior reporter who had left Doncaster years ago? The *Doncaster Chronicle* solved the problem neatly by headlining the story:

ANTHONY BARBER'S BROTHER STABBED

Then Macmillan gave Tony his first big break in politics. The *Daily Mail* rightly felt that his preferment should be recorded, but who on earth had heard of this young MP, coming from a constituency in the frozen North? They solved their problem equally neatly with the headline:

NOEL BARBER'S
BROTHER GETS
BIG NEW JOB

For those of us who tired of work (or to be more precise, of being together in some benighted spot, waiting for orders) there were games. For me, tennis.

Wherever I travelled I carried my racquet. I have played tennis all over the world, including one set which for length beat even the most famous marathon between my old friend Budge Patty and Drobny. My game, which was a doubles, never reached the end of the first set. We drew at forty-seven games all, when good light stopped play, though I blush to admit that the game was rigged to end in a draw. This was during the Vietnam War, and it had to be rigged for one of the players was Duong Van Minh – 'Big Minh' as he was known – then jostling to become premier of Vietnam. So was his opponent, and this was a serious matter in a country where highly placed officials who lost at tennis also lost face.

I had played singles several times with one of the local correspondents; the two politicians (both in a position to grant or refuse interviews) were mad on tennis, which was always played at Le Cercle Sportif in Saigon at 6.30 a.m., finishing the moment the sun hit the courts around eight o'clock. Would I care to make up a four?

'The only thing,' said my colleague diffidently, 'is that if either of us beats the other minister, that means a closed door until the government topples. Could we – well—?' I took the point.

Never engage in a ploy like this. It may be a simple matter deliberately to lose a match, but to fix a draw in a game where anyone can make unforced errors is an exhausting mental test, specially when two of the players are going all out for every shot.

If Big Minh won his serve, then the chances were that I had to lose mine, and on one occasion when we were in the lead – I forget the score, but it was in the region of 29–28 – I unthinkingly served an ace to give us a 40–15 lead. Much too perilous because if our opponents muffed the next shot, perhaps by hitting the service return into the net, we would have won.

Luckily Minh's partner was quick to realise the danger and shouted out as I aced him, 'My God, Noel! That was the most glaring foot fault I've ever seen.'

With suitable apologies I conceded the point and honour was saved.

In between the fun and games – these are really what one wants to remember – there were moments of tragedy, none more terrible than the Hungarian uprising of 1956 when I managed not only to get *into* the country, but was able to get my story *out*. One or two correspondents were already in Budapest when the battle for freedom started, but could not file because it was impossible to cable or telephone, and even if one had a car, there was no petrol.

When the fighting started I happened to be in London. I flew to Vienna, and at the airport was met by Laurie Davis, our stringer, who had found me a hired car with Austrian registration plates (we had to put down £1,000 deposit) and before making for the Hungarian frontier, I loaded it with ten jerricans of petrol. But I knew that once inside Hungary the Russians would search my car and confiscate any petrol. Fortunately I knew just where to hide it.

All foreign correspondents need luck and by sheer chance I had motored through Hungary only two weeks previously on my way back from an assignment to see Tito in Belgrade. I had spent my last night in Hungary at a small hotel in Hegyeshalom, near the Austrian frontier, choosing it only because I had been told that the *patron* served the finest fresh good liver in all Hungary. I remembered the owner as I managed to bribe and argue my way across the frontier, and once in Hungary I made straight for Hegyeshalom, woke up the innkeeper, and left all my spare petrol with him.

From the moment I drove towards Budapest I became engulfed in a dark and wicked hell, for once the Russians had decided to stamp out Hungary's pitiful bid for freedom they were merciless. I reached Buda around midnight and found myself with insurgents behind a barricade of upturned railway coaches; we were defending ourselves against Russian tank and mortar fire from the Chain Bridge spanning the Danube. Before dawn I helped to bury two teenagers who died in my arms. I saw nearly a hundred unarmed youngsters mowed down by machine-gun fire in a village square, and scores of civilians butchered in a demonstration near the Parliament building.

Though there were no cable facilities, I was so sickened that (quite apart from my instincts as a reporter) I would have walked to the frontier if necessary to let the world know details of the carnage around me. Thanks to the supplies of hidden petrol I was able to drive the hundred miles or so to the frontier almost daily and throw my photographs and dispatches over the frontier pole to Jeffrey Blyth, an old colleague on the *Mail*, who was waiting for me on the other side – in Austria. (He had been sent to help because I realised that if I once left Hungarian soil I might not be able to get back in again.)

Each day I filled my tank with petrol and drove back to Budapest. I was searched a dozen times a day, but all went well until, at the end of the first week, I was driving quietly towards the Duna Hotel in Budapest when a Russian soldier opened up with a sub-machine-gun. I received two bullets in the head, but managed to reach a freedom fighters' hospital where I had fifty-two stitches in the head (alas, the anaesthetic had run out by then). I was there for a week, before Jeffrey found me – by then the frontier was easier to cross. Miraculously the battered car was still in running order, and on hearing that the Russians were looking for me (my eyewitness dispatches having received much publicity), I fled the hospital in my pyjamas, drove along the snow-covered roads, and finally across the mine fields to a lonely spot where I was able to escape into Austria.

Yet when I think of Hungary, it is not so much of the terrible things I saw, but of a letter I received much later, from a young Hungarian called Denes, who had been a great help to me, travelling with me each day. I begged him to escape with me when I fled, but he refused, so I gave him everything I had – my last cigarettes and chocolate, my pens, some books, and what was left of my money and travellers' cheques.

After we said good-bye I heard nothing from him until seven years later, when a letter arrived at the *Daily Mail*. It had been smuggled out of Hungary by a friend; it told of a miserable existence. Denes could not find regular work because of rumours that he had 'helped the West'; he had been hungry and ill. The letter ended:

Excuse my disturbing you, but after years I had an opportunity to have your travellers' cheques sent to a friend in Germany, because even when I was nearly starving, I didn't dare to cash them. But now the cheques are very old and he can no longer change them, so my friend is sending them to you, in the hope that you can send him the cash instead, and he will get it to me.

That to me, sums up the continuing story of communism.

I might never have really seen Dr Simondy, the man who saved my life, for at times the pain when stitching me up was so intense that I lost consciousness. But years later, a 'miracle' arrived. As a complete surprise to me, I was chosen to appear in *This is Your Life*. All those years and I had no contact with him. Then some patient researcher had tracked him down. We spoke for the first time – and I saw him properly for the first time.

As a change from the derring-do dateline, I was occasionally allowed to indulge in assignments in which I would cover a story in the lap of luxury, with three good meals a day, all the *vino* one could drink, and all for free. Not only free, but with an extra financial bonus thrown in after I had persuaded the *Daily Mail* to let me have a flat daily allowance for expenses instead of having to spend hours trying to itemise them.

They agreed to allow me £15 a day to look after myself when away from home – a lot of money in those days. I did not have to account for it, just indicate where I had been. Out of this sum I had to pay hotels, taxis, tips, food, everything except travel and hire of cars (as apart from taxis). I had of course credit cards for cabling and air travel.

The *Mail* benefited too, because I needed all the money I could earn to look after my polyglot family, and the new arrangement not only prevented me from complaining when away from Switzerland for lengthy periods, but encouraged me to volunteer for anti-social missions. After all, when I arrived home after spending ninety days in the Antarctic, Titina had, as expected, disbursed all the salary I had earned during that period, but I was able to put in a one-line expenses sheet, 'To Antarctica at £15 per day, £1395'. (If anyone notes a discrepancy in these figures, the amount was arrived at by charging for ninety days in the Antarctic, plus three nights paid for by BOAC when my flight to New Zealand was delayed in Perth.)

Typical of comfortable datelines was the time when I was accredited to the US Pacific Fleet for a tour, and arrived to make my number with the admiral in Honolulu. There was some delay, so for two weeks I was housed in the BOQ (Bachelor Officers' Quarters) with a free ride to the beach every day, all at a cost of $1.50 a day (drinks extra). Each noon a naval officer phoned me to apologise for the delay, reaching me on a telephone extension plugged into a post on Waikiki Beach, and each day I soothed him, 'Don't worry. I'm sure you're doing all you can.'

I really didn't mind. Though Honolulu, with its sky-scrapers and blistered macadam roads, could be mistaken for Blackpool, and the famous narrow strip of Waikiki Beach has about the same allure as the edge of the Serpentine, Hawaii is an ideal place in which to indulge in the great American pastime of people-watching. The young people of the Hawaiian Islands are the most exquisite in the world, compounded of all the most beautiful races in the Pacific, a scintillating cast set against a backdrop of dreamy, romantic music.

I must have had to shout when speaking on the plugged-in phone one morning, for when I raise my voice my faint Northern accent becomes more pronounced. It was certainly noticeable to a blonde lady of a certain age (but with a very trim figure) who was sunbathing near by, because she jumped up and came straight towards me.

'Baa goom, lad,' she cried in a mock Yorkshire accent. 'Ah do believe tha cooms fra Yorkshire.'

Which was how I met Dorothy Mackaill, who had emigrated from Hull (where once the Barbers lived) to become one of the Goldwyn Girls, then a star of silent films, and later a respected retired member of the Beverly Hills set. She had not only lived in Hull, she had lived in Anlaby Road. Number 724. The Barbers, in those early days, had lived at 722. A right neighbourly meeting.

Dorothy was on holiday, and so were some friends of hers, all of us staying in the same hotel. Which is how I started a friendship which has lasted to this day with James and Gloria Stewart and their children. When we met I wrote in my diary,

Dinner with Jimmy and Gloria Stewart. He is so like his film self it is almost like being at the cinema. Long,

gangling, very shy until the second or third drink, but
great fun. Wears glasses often, thinning on top, a grey
rim on his hair. Dined at The Willows with the children,
a restaurant with a dozen different rooms, all furnished
in bamboo, grouped around heavy woods and very large
ponds filled with fish. Great fun for Jimmy's nine-year-
old twin daughters who started feeding the carp with
bread but became so excited they ended up throwing in
large lumps of cherry pie.

Jimmy drove us all back to the hotel in his station wagon,
the entire family singing the 'Stewart theme song'. I noted
the powerful lyrics:

> Don't cry lady, I'll buy your stinking violets,
> Don't cry lady, I'll buy your pencils too.
> Don't cry lady, take off those old dark glasses.
> Why, hullo mother! I knew it was you.

The de luxe Honolulu dateline lasted only two weeks, but
I made the most of another one, this time in Europe after
Elsa Maxwell had been asked by the Greek Government
to promote tourism. It was a challenge she was delighted
to accept – but only on her own terms.

Not for Elsa the gimmick of the London hostess who
arranges a charity ball in aid of the poor where guests salve
their consciences by paying £10 each to guzzle half-cold
soup, half-warm chicken, half-melted ice cream, washed
down with half-sweet white wine just off the boil. A true
professional, Elsa put all her weight (which literally as well
as figuratively was not inconsiderable) behind the project.
She decided to invite a hundred influential millionaires on
a two-week cruise around the Greek islands.

Firstly, she borrowed a ship – a large ship, with a normal
capacity for four hundred passengers, which allowed enough breathing space in first class for even the most pam-
pered millionaire, while the tourist class would in theory
be left unoccupied, but in practice turned out to be very

useful for those unable to resist the lure of illicit shipboard romances, not necessarily heterosexual.

It promised to be the ultimate way of having a good time in order to do good. But in the event only ninety-eight millionaires were accommodated, for when I heard about the proposed voyage, I said to Elsa, 'Come on, darling, couldn't you drop two of your millionaire friends and include Titina and myself? The *Daily Mail* would love the exclusive story.' So it was arranged, and the *crème de la crème* of café society gathered for a huge ball given in their honour at the Palazzo Volpi on the Grand Canal in Venice, from where we would depart.

Stavros Niarchos – whose house in Paris I had visited from time to time – was in Venice, and on the eve of our departure asked a dozen of us on board his black three-masted *Creole*. She is one of the most aesthetically perfect yachts in the world; Niarchos once told me that he would like to be buried from her at sea. (Alas, she is now discarded in favour of a new girl friend, the *Atlantis*.)

Niarchos is a living proof of the old saw that wealth does not necessarily bring happiness. He might always have been able to command anything that money can buy, but he cannot bring back two wives who both died from overdoses. Yet, as though cocking a snook at fate, Niarchos at least has made an effort to try and enjoy life more than his lugubrious rival Onassis. For though Ari did achieve a certain kind of happiness, he rarely displayed any sense of humour, whereas Niarchos, with his almost puckish face – rather like a Greek Beaverbrook – retained a wicked sense of fun, and prepared to illustrate it on this occasion.

He was not sailing with us, so after farewell drinks with his guests, who included Princess Maria Pia of Italy, and her husband, Prince Alexander of Yugoslavia, we set sail for Corfu, where we had been invited to a reception given by the mayor and local dignitaries.

This might seem like a dull chore, but not so, for when we trooped ashore into the mayor's parlour, the entire staff appeared to be drunk. Half a dozen waiters and waitresses stumbled around slopping glasses of champagne, whisky and Greek retsina, or dropping canapés off precariously balanced plates. Several elderly and sedate millionairesses were approached by leering waiters, and one girl with a thick slash of lipstick, and a face hardly visible behind a mask of powder, handed me some smoked salmon with her fingers, and then planted a kiss on my cheek.

It took half an hour for the drachma to drop. Early in the day, while we were at sea, Niarchos had transferred his guests from the *Creole* to his private four-engined plane and flown them to Corfu. Long before we arrived he had commandeered the mayor's parlour, and dressed up his guests as waiters and waitresses.

She plants a firm kiss, does Maria Pia.

13

THE RULING CLASS

MARIA PIA WAS a royal, but I prefer royals to be kept in their place – which should be on a comfortable throne in a pleasant palace, sufficiently ostentatious to impress African tribal chiefs elevated beyond their normal station, attract envious tourists whose ancestors lopped off crowned heads, yet not be flashy enough to encourage local commies to revolt.

Above all royals must be regal, for they are the stars of a nation's pantomime, and since it costs a great deal of money to keep the show on the road, they must never step out of character and destroy the illusion. A queen riding down the Mall on a bicycle is about as silly as a baker delivering his dozen in thirteen royal coaches.

Up to the time of writing I have not met our Queen, though a friend did once try to flog me his invitation for a garden party at Buckingham Palace. I have, however, had more luck with others, and the most delightful of all was without doubt King Hussein of Jordan, whose private papers I helped to put in order so that he could write his memoirs. I had previously interviewed the King on occasion, always taking the trouble to send him clippings of the resultant articles. (It has long been a habit of mine: it is little trouble, and gives many people passing pleasure.) When the idea came to me in 1960 that the King's life story would make a gripping book, I sent him a 1000-word cable couched in such friendly terms that even his most suspicious servitors would be afraid to hide it from him. A few days later he cabled a laconic reply, 'IT'S A GRAND IDEA.'

I was delighted because, apart from the challenge, it

meant that for once Titina and the children could come
and stay with me in Jordan without any fear of my suddenly
being sent half-way across the world. The *Daily Mail*
was equally pleased because in exchange for my modest
services, the King had agreed to give them first-serial rights
in his book.

Within weeks the family Barber was in Amman, installed
in a villa with a pool in the garden, and an excellent cook.
The King also provided us with a car and a sergeant driver.
Hussein was charming, with a highly developed sense of
humour; a generous, honest and simple man who took it
in turns with his then English wife Muna to cook breakfast
in the modest house where they lived in preference to the
ostentatious royal palace.

Each day, after the affairs of state had ended – sometimes at 3 p.m., sometimes 11 p.m. – the King came to my
villa, where we worked until he was tired; on the following
morning I worked on the previous night's tapes. All went
well until Abdullah, my cook had a day off. Around
lunchtime, much earlier than expected, the bell rang.

Titina was out shopping. I was sunning myself by the
pool, and the first thing I heard was the piping voice of
Simonetta, who can't have been more than four, crying,
'Hello, King!' I received His Majesty in my bathing cos-
tume.

'I'm starved,' said the King. 'You pop a shirt on while
I go into the kitchen and scramble some eggs.' And the
King cooked a meal fit for a king.

He had come early because we faced some problems
with chapter six, particularly pages fourteen and fifteen.
Finally, after a difficult afternoon, the King bundled up
the thirty or so pages on which he had been working, and
said, 'I'll take them home with me and then we'll go
through them again tomorrow.'

'Remember it's the only copy,' I said anxiously. 'Don't
lose them.'

But he did – well, nearly. He drove off in his Thunderbird
to his helicopter pad for the ten-minute flight to his house,

and as I watched him fly over my villa, I saw a cloud of confetti scatter through the blue skies. Chapter six.

Fortunately, monarchs who survive in the Middle East take care to instil a sense of absolute discipline in their police force, knowing that once that goes, they go. In an instant the King was talking on his air-to-ground transmitter. Hundreds of Amman police tore out into the dusty, hilly, ochre streets of the capital, all eyes turned upwards to the slowly descending, swirling pieces of paper. All normal duties were forgotten. Traffic was halted, the curious shoved on to the sidewalks. And it says much for police discipline that every sheet of paper except three – among them, alas, pages fourteen and fifteen – was grasped in eager hands.

The King never did recover those two pages with their vital message. Even worse, neither of us could remember what they contained. Not to worry. With a couple of deft lines the King linked up pages thirteen and sixteen, and no one missed the pages over which we had wrestled so long and in vain.

The King had – still has – a razor-sharp mind, and while I was spending the best part of five months working with him he only slipped up once, forcing me to say 'No thank you, sir' to the offer of a large gold watch.

The Middle East just about keeps Switzerland in the gold watch industry. Say good-bye to an Arab prince, and the chances are that he will produce a watch emblazoned with his crest as a farewell memento. Hussein was no exception. A month or so after I first arrived in Jordan, I had to fly to London to undertake some research. The King wished me good-bye in the traditional manner, with a spanking gold Rolex watch. Overwhelmed, I accepted it without a moment's hesitation, even though I was only leaving for a week or so.

Months later, when I finally left Amman, a city I really love, I went to the palace to bid the King farewell. Out came the royal handshake. And, yes, out came another gold Rolex.

'But, sir,' I protested, 'you've already given me *one*.'

'Did I?' Kings never look confused, but Hussein was slightly taken aback. 'Very remiss of me,' and then with his famous grin, he added, 'Is there anything else I can do for you instead?'

As it happened, there was. I had bought ten large brown garden pots, each one about two feet tall and looking rather like Italian olive jars, for our garden.

'Well, sir,' I began. 'If the Jordanian Air Force is sending a plane to Europe could they take those pots for me?'

'I don't think any of our planes *will* be flying to Europe in the near future,' said the King. 'Better take them with you as extra baggage. I'll arrange for someone to crate them.' Then he added laconically, 'And I'll tell BOAC to send the bill for any overweight to me.'

Which is just what happened. I had bought the pots in the local market, and at 10p each I considered the capital outlay of £1 for ten modest. The bill for the overweight came to just under £200.

While we were living in Amman Sam Spiegel's production of the film *Lawrence of Arabia* was being shot in southern Jordan, with David Lean directing. I had met Sam once or twice at parties, but in view of the bitterness between Arab and Jew he was the last man I expected to see in Jordan, even though he is very, very powerful and expects to get his own way as a matter of course. But there he was, the only Jew, surrounded by Arabs, drinking coffee on the terrace of the Philadelphia Hotel in Amman. Sam is hardly noted for his Arab cast of countenance, and my first thought was that he had been spirited past the Mandelbaum Gate (then the frontier in Jerusalem) and my second was that some fanatical Arabs insist on cutting off certain protruding parts of Christian and Jewish bodies and I would have hated Sam to be caught with his pants down.

'Don't worry.' Mr Spiegel bit the end off a large cigar. 'I'm just on my way to see the boys shooting *Lawrence*' – for which film he had arranged to hire (at a hefty cost) a

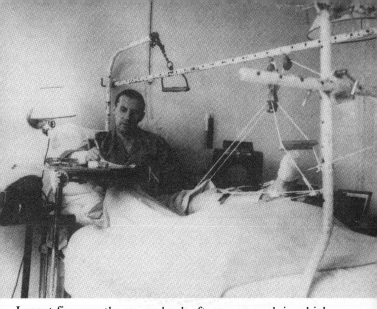

I spent five months on my back after a car crash in which four people died

My father Jack with Noel, Tony and Ken after receiving the CBE in 1958

Something of value: I spent all my spare time painting

Ambushed on the way to the relief of Tizi-Ouzli in Morocco. (NB terrified by loan of pistol)

On patrol near the Yemen frontier

Poles apart: Welcoming Ed Hillary to the South Pole, and (*below*) my colleague Emmwood has some fun in the *Daily Mail* during a spell I spent living on an iceberg near the North Pole

Clark Gable warns me, 'Never trust a woman'. Flying with King Hussein in Jordan. NB carries a ceremonial scarf offered as a token of friendship by the Dalai Lama

With Marlene Dietrich in the Bois de Boulogne, Paris

Here tomorrow, gone today – farewell to Titina before
another assignment

A flying Noel Barber

Fame (it's all relative) for NB

large part of the Jordanian Army and most of its camels, so that he was, after all, only protecting his investment.

I didn't see him again until the day I flew back to London with my watch. He was at the airport with some colleagues, so as I passed I waved and said, 'Cheers, Sam. I'm off to London.'

On the insistence of the King's servitors I was taken on board the BOAC aircraft before the other passengers, and then, when they were seated, lap-straps fastened, the engines were warmed up and we seemed all set for take-off. Suddenly there was a kerfuffle. The steward started to pull the heavy lever that opened one of the doors. A stewardess's voice piped, 'Will Mr Barber please make himself known.'

When I raised a hand she came to my seat and said, 'There's someone who has an important message for you so we're holding back the plane' – adding as I prepared to disembark, 'No, no, he's coming on board now.'

What had I done to displease the King? For who else would have the temerity to stop an aircraft at the moment it was preparing to taxi from the apron? As I wondered, the steps were trundled up and there, framed in the small doorway, were the massive shoulders of Sam Spiegel.

The stewardess pointed out my seat. Sam came and leant over me. 'I just wanted to say good-bye,' he said.

'Is that all?' I gasped.

'No, not really,' he chuckled. 'I also wanted to demonstrate our power in an Arab country.'

It needed a right royal gesture by King Hussein to allow Sam Spiegel into his country, but then Hussein has remained ruler of Jordan because he is tough, has both feet on the ground, and doesn't give a damn for anyone if he believes he is right. (Ask Glubb Pasha.) A supreme realist like his grandfather who was assassinated by his side, Hussein was always hoping that the Arabs and Jews could somehow make peace. Which was why Nasser wasted so much time and money trying to kill Hussein – and once, while I was in the palace, very nearly succeeded.

The King has always suffered from sinus trouble, which he alleviates with nose drops. One evening as we were leaving to attend a theatrical performance in the magnificent forum, built by the Romans and seating six thousand, he went into the bathroom to get some drops. By the grace of the Prophet he spilled some of the liquid from the dropper. It landed on one of the taps and within seconds had burned off the chromium. Nasser's agents had switched his medicine, substituting that hackneyed standby sulphuric acid.

That was the night I said to the King, 'One day they'll get you. I know you'd hate to leave Jordan, but—'

'That's what they want me to do,' he replied. 'But I'd rather die here than be an ex-king living in a villa on the French Riviera.'

By the time I was working with the King, the Barber family had moved from Switzerland to London, because the *Mail* felt it important for me to be nearer the centre of operations. I was very sad to leave the old farm, but, as so often happens, it turned out for the best. In London I was in the thick of things, so that when I was not travelling, I could meet publishers, editors, television producers, and was stimulated to work much harder. Titina loved England. We were lucky too, for when we left one beautiful house, we found another equally delightful, Turner's studio in Cheyne Walk, and it was to this author's modest home that King Hussein came to spend an evening after the book was finished.

Musty, Titina's son, collected a dozen assorted girls, I bought a dozen assorted LP records and we danced until 5 a.m. – with one interlude. Around midnight the King, suddenly very serious, beckoned for the music to stop. He took me into the corridor behind our large living room. An aide handed him a square flat box of the size and purple hue that in every country identifies it instantly as a repository for medals or decorations. I was very touched when the King invested me with one of his country's decorations.

Almost immediately the aide produced another identical square flat purple box. The King asked Titina to step forward. I knew that Titina would be honoured, though I also knew that, being an Italian realist, she would be wondering if she would ever have occasion to wear a medal.

'We all feel,' explained the King, 'that you deserve some sort of recognition because you had to be away from home for so long.' At which His Majesty beckoned loftily to the aide to hand him the box, opened it and took out – no, not a medal but a magnificent diamond brooch.

We went to bed around dawn, the brooch propped up on Titina's bedside table. When she woke and sipped her first coffee of the day, she took one long look at it, and turned to me. 'Isn't it wonderful,' she sighed blissfully, 'to think that I didn't have to do anything for it.'

Hussein is a real king, imperious on occasions, a man of principle, yet kind and considerate. But I have never witnessed a more imperious act by a ruler than when I attended a party given by the Sultan of Johore (he who had been so generous to me with his lady friends). Very shortly after we first met, I was invited to the palace again, but on this occasion in very different circumstances, for the Sultan was still at loggerheads with the British.

Ibrahim not only *looked* every inch a ruler, but in Johore he *was* every inch a ruler. His fiat, however, did not extend across the Causeway to the Crown colony of Singapore – and the prettiest Chinese, Malay, Filipino and Indian girls for miles around. The colony at that time was governed by the particularly obtuse Sir Shenton Thomas, who in 1938 was incensed with the Sultan on several counts, including the apparently accurate rumour that he had won a huge bet at Singapore races by substituting an unknown dark horse disguised with a coat of paint. But most of all Thomas was irked by the offhand way in which the Sultan had recently divorced his wife, a worthy Scotswoman who had tried in vain to curb her husband's extra-marital activities. The divorce proceedings were simple. The Sultan, in front of witnesses, cried the equivalent of 'Get out!' three times, and his wife went – to be replaced, before long, by the cabaret dancer Lydia Hill.

Sir Shenton, anxious to administer a public rebuke, waited for an opportune moment. The Sultan gave an annual reception for Malay rulers, to which, according to custom, all the nobs of the British Civil Service were also invited (together with the editor of the local paper). These invitations were much sought after by the British, but Lydia Hill was in residence and Sir Shenton pounced, forbidding any members of the Singapore government to attend, coupling this with strongly worded requests to business leaders (who needed to be on good terms with the government) to boycott the party.

I suffered from no such shackles, but as I munched my canapés I stood out like a whiter-than-white soap powder while the Sultan's brow grew blacker and blacker. No other Britons arrived. Around midnight he looked, glowering, over the palace golf course bathed in moonlight – a course used for decades by perspiring Britishers – and came to a decision of right royal authority. He ordered out the Army.

The prospect of an armed uprising was stimulating, but short-lived. Two platoons of troops shuffled round to the back of the palace and indented for spades and other gardening implements, before marching off into the night. With the dawn came Ibrahim's revenge. Cheerfully the first members of the British colony arrived for their morning nine holes on one of the few golf courses for miles around – only to find every fairway and green planted with shrubs.

Kings live in a real world, but ladies and gentlemen of the blood royal who no longer have thrones they can call their own tend to dwell in a more rarefied atmosphere. When

Titina and I had decided to marry, the Windsors (to our astonishment) gave us an engagement party – a charming gesture and a charming party. With his usual impeccable manners, the Duke took Titina aside after dinner and talked to her in his excellent Italian. From time to time I watched them. Was she looking appehensive? Was the Duke discussing politics with a girl whose political convictions are limited to a firm belief that the difference between right and wrong in politics is really the difference between right and left?

Not so, I learned later. Having discovered that Titina's family had known, if slightly, King Umberto of Italy, the Duke was inquiring anxiously for news about his colleague in the 'ex-' club. How *was* Umberto? Was he happy in Estoril, that rather dreary Portuguese resort where he had set up his court? Surely he must be bored? Was it true that the old boy was still doing his *petit point*?

Years later Charles Forte gave a large dinner in London for ex-King Umberto. The guests were seated at a dozen or so small tables, and because Titina's mother had been an Ambassadress, Titina was seated at ex-King Umberto's table. After inquiring about her family, Umberto bombarded Titina with almost the same questions about the Duke of Windsor. Was it true that 'poor David' wasn't well? Was he bored by Paris? Was it true that he played drums in a night club? And didn't Titina think it a pity the Queen refused to bend a bit towards 'poor Wallis'?

The harmless assumption, by two ex-kings in two different capitals, that we were all bosom chums together – not intimate, you understand, but certainly close enough friends to borrow a pint of milk if one of us ran out – was slightly disconcerting, and was presumably based on the mistaken assumption that Titina was an *ex gratia* member of the 'ex-' club.

It used to be said in the good old days that the difference between an Oxford and a Cambridge man was that the former walked into a room as if he owned it, and the latter as though he didn't give a damn *who* owned it. A similar difference separates the attitudes of kings out of a job from military commanders living on a pension and the past.

Ex-kings, born and bred in palaces they do not really own, molly-coddled from birth in purple swaddling clothes, display a charming, happy-go-lucky 'Cambridge' indifference to their immediate surroundings, perhaps because they know they would not be there if someone had not previously cased the joint. Or possibly the indifference is born out of being ordered what to do from birth to death.

Ex-generals are a very different breed, for they were used to *giving* orders, and old habits die hard. They enter a room, eyes darting, as though deciding whether their quartermaster was right to have commandeered it. None more so than Field-Marshal Montgomery, whom I met several times in Paris, and with whom I maintained a pleasant, if desultory, correspondence over the years, each one of his letters in green ink usually asking me some small favour. I liked Monty. He was vain, quirky and bossy, but I hate to see him the target of ill-informed criticism.

The last time I saw Monty I invited him to lunch – on Armistice Day, 1963 – at the Empress in Berkeley Street, where I could be certain that Negri, the manager, would install us at the large corner table well away from any other guests, and their cigarette smoke. I still have the notes I made immediately we parted company. Nothing very important, but Monty never stepped out of character.

'Good staff work,' he barked as I led him to the table. 'Glad you said lunch. I'd have refused if you'd asked me for dinner.'

Negri appeared.

'Thick soup,' Monty barked again. 'Anything thick, don't care what the flavour is, followed by two lamb chops with *épinards*' – and then, as though to explain to multilingual Negri – 'that's spinach, you know.' He drank a glass of orange juice, topped off the meal with an apple, and 'Coffee, half milk, in a large cup'.

I only saw Monty as a fascinated observer on rare

occasions, but what a hell of a tyrant he must have been
on parade. Perhaps that is why the Eighth Army worshipped him.

An odd fellow. Once in Paris he phoned me at the *Mail*
inviting me to lunch at NATO headquarters in Fontaine-
bleau later in the week. 'I'm going to see Mao in China,'
he . . . (What's another word for 'barked'?) 'I gather
you've written a book on the Far East. Come round – I
want to pick your brains.'

My knowledge of China was strictly limited. I had not
been there since 1938 and everything had changed especially in the Peking I had visited before the war. I did
have a few notes in my diary, but not containing the kind
of material likely to appeal to Monty – the addresses of
divers dives, together with restaurants more likely to serve
bears' paws than lamb chops; and even all these must have
been swept away. I boned up on the Yangtze River, the
Forbidden City in Peking, and Chairman Mao, and a few
days later drove out to a lunch spartan enough to prove
that though an army may march on its stomach, its officers
don't.

Which terrified junior officer, brusquely told to find a
Far Eastern expert, had perchance read a book I once
wrote on the Orient, so bad that I have been trying ever
since to find the last copies and burn them? How on earth
had Monty taken this man's word for it without reading
the book to check? Perhaps Monty didn't read a great
deal.

Anyway, I never got a word in at lunch. My job was to
sit as an expert while Monty explained in detail the plans
he had already formulated for his trip. And since I did not
have the faintest clue what he was really talking about, I
could not even disagree. A few 'sage' nods seemed to suit
the occasion, and when I left Monty was as pleased as
punch – and convinced that his plans were sound simply
because one of the greatest living Chinese scholars [*sic*]
had agreed with every one of them.

Monty was as vain as a peacock, but he was not the only vain man among the ruling class, for power not only corrupts (on occasion) it breeds vanity more swiftly than any infectious disease known to man. Marshal Ky, for two years prime minister of South Vietnam, told me once in Saigon that at the Honolulu conference President Johnson invited him back to his hotel suite for a drink, finally beckoning him into his bedroom with a whispered, 'I've got something for you.'

Ky, a young, dashing fighter pilot at heart, wondered what secrets Johnson was about to impart. Once in the bedroom the American President handed Ky a large photograph, saying, 'You'll see I've signed it personally for you.'

During the Korean war President Syngman Rhee, once a lift boy at the Ritz in New York, behaved in much the same manner after I had spent an hour interviewing him in his camouflaged, net-covered villa outside Seoul. 'I hope you write a favourable article about me,' he said, adding, 'Wait a moment; I have something for you.'

A bribe? A fat wad of notes? No such luck. 'I've signed it personally for you,' said the President, handing me his photograph.

With President Hastings Banda of Malawi, I for once in my life got the better of a politician in a verbal battle – no easy task, for by the nature of their calling politicians can usually outsmart any amateur verbally, especially one like myself who can never strike while the irony is hot, but always thinks of the perfect retort while fuming in the bath the following morning. However, without undue vanity I think I can say that on this occasion I left Banda nonplussed by my final remark.

Malawi is perhaps the most beautiful country in Africa. When it was still called Nyasaland, I had once spent three weeks attending a conference at Salima, on the shores of Lake Malawi, sharing a *rondval* with a bright young reporter from Reuters, a man who later decided that if the pen is mightier than the sword, the face is mightier than the pen. He moved over to TV. His name is Sandy Gall.

Years later I returned, Nyasaland now being independent Malawi. I had decided to interview President Banda, a chore I approached with some distaste as he is a difficult man to interview.

Just before my allotted time expired, I thanked him for his courtesy, and said, 'It's a long time since I last met you, Mr President. Do you remember the evening when we had supper together?'

'Supper?' he cried. 'We never had supper together.'

'But, sir, it was here at your house in Blantyre, with Donald Wise of the *Daily Express*. You were just carving the ham when the British troops came and arrested you.'

If the President of Malawi had still been holding that carving knife, I might be writing left-handed now.

During the same trip in the early seventies I interviewed Ian Smith, prime minister of Rhodesia, but only because of a wildly improbable misunderstanding on the part of Rhodesians, isolated from the world, who found it impossible to believe that I could be visiting Salisbury without *some* motive. In fact, I was passing through on my way to Bulawayo to research an article for the *Reader's Digest*, and decided to look up a few old friends. Besides, it was the Rhodesian summer and the streets were looking beautiful with the large mauve trumpet-shaped flowers of jacaranda trees in full bloom. I was in Salisbury for one reason only – because I loved the place, and said as much when I was interviewed at the airport on my arrival.

At the time yet another effort was being made to establish some *rapport* between Whitehall and Salisbury. Late that same evening, after dinner at Meikles Hotel, the telephone rang and a friend in the government simply said, 'Glad you're here. You'll be hearing from us in the morning.' When I asked how he knew of my arrival – for the newspapers had not yet appeared – he laughed, 'We're at war, you know. We've got a very good espionage system.'

Shortly after breakfast the following morning, another

friend in Government information asked me on the phone, almost too casually, 'I imagine you'd like to see Mr Smith?'

Though I was on this occasion working for the *Digest*, not in Salisbury on business, I never refuse to meet anyone who intrigues me. But I was even more startled when my friend added, 'The Prime Minister is expecting you at eleven o'clock. In view of the delicate nature of the talks now taking place, I hope you don't mind if we tape the interview. Don't worry, I'll have it typed for you.'

I expected nothing more than a social call, with possibly a glass of sanctions-busting sherry, for I had met Mr Smith before. But to my astonishment, he talked frankly and at great length about the problems facing Rhodesia. He suggested possible lines of solution that I knew had never been printed before. I began to sniff headlines. Finally, the interview over, the tape was transcribed in another room, and the glass of sherry appeared.

Smith's first small-talk question was curious: 'How well do you know Prime Minister Heath?'

I had to admit that I hardly moved in political circles, though he had once been to our home for drinks.

'Well, here's to your brother Tony,' added Smith. 'I've always admired him.'

Until that moment I had completely forgotten that brother Tony was Chancellor of the Exchequer. Nor did Tony have the faintest idea that I was in Africa. But to this day (as I learned later) the Rhodesians firmly believe that Tony and Ted Heath sent me out privately and unofficially to sound out Ian Smith's views.

I telephoned the story to the *Daily Mail*, and when it made the splash I felt ten years younger.

Politicians and others in public life share one fascinating trait which must take years of practice to develop. It is the royal memory – but with a subtle difference. The royals are supposed to have prodigious memories and never forget a face or a name. But they are the faces or names of people *they have met*. People in the public eye go one stage further. They have mastered to an uncanny degree the ability to remember the faces of people they have *never* met, and do not know. I discovered this on the trip to Rhodesia when I interviewed Ian Smith.

I was sitting in the lounge at Meikles Hotel, when suddenly I saw Hughie Green walking towards me. Jumping up, I held out my hand and cried, 'Hughie Green! Fancy meeting you here' – adding, as I always do, an identifying phrase to avoid the inevitable blank look. 'You remember me – Noel Barber of the *Daily Mail*.'

Two hands grasped mine firmly, the famous smile creased its way across the famous face, and with the enthusiasm of an old and true friend, Hughie cried, 'But, Noel, what the hell are *you* doing here?'

Now this makes me sound damn silly, but we had never met before and I was not trying to be clever. I had seen Hughie Green's face so often on television that when suddenly it appeared in front of me in faraway Rhodesia, I must have skipped a dozen thought processes so swiftly that the computer ticking inside my brain received wrong information, and gave out an answer, 'Look, there's an old friend.'

It would have been unfair to disabuse Mr Green after he had behaved so politely, but what fascinated me was the speed with which he changed gears to adapt to the classical showbiz situation where fan confronts celebrity. I wasn't a fan (though I admire his courage and professionalism), I was suffering from a brain disorder, but his reaction was so instant, so controlled, that I determined one day to try out the ploy deliberately on some famous man or woman, merely to discover if this reaction is standard among celebrities.

The occasion came in London when I was a guest at the 'Authors of the Year' party at the Martini Terrace, on the top floor of New Zealand House. Most of the authors were *really* famous, and there was also a star-studded cast of celebrity guests, including George Brown, holding forth, glass in hand.

'It always seems a bit odd to me,' said Titina, not actually complaining, 'that you never seem to know any of these famous people – look at the crowd around George Brown.'

For a split second Hughie Green's image appeared in front of me. 'George *Brown*,' I cried, changing colours. 'But darling, I've known George for ages. It never entered my head that you wanted to meet him. Come on!'

I pushed forward, and varying my identification slightly to suit the victim, I said jovially, 'George! How well you look. You remember me – Noel Barber of the *Mail*, Tony Barber's brother.'

'My God! *You*, Noel. What have you been *doing* with yourself lately?' By the end of the evening, George Brown, who hadn't the faintest idea who I was (apart from being Tony's brother), turned to Titina and said, 'You know, I think Noel's lost a bit of weight. Suits him.'

Nice guy, George. I must get someone to introduce us.

14

DISTANT PLACES

MY JOURNEY TO the South Pole in 1957 – 'First Briton since
Scott' and all that jazz – excited some comment at the time.
I had gone to Antarctica to report on the Fuchs-Hillary
Transantarctic expedition. It was not for me to disabuse
Daily Mail readers by revealing that I might never have
reached the Pole had my penis not stuck to the frozen
metal of a lavatory pan in the communal loo at McMurdo
Sound, the American base near the Ross Ice Shelf, 826
miles from the Pole.

It was one thing to reach McMurdo – by plane when the
ice held, or by ice-breaker from New Zealand – but it was
much more difficult to get from McMurdo to the Pole,
because landing conditions were difficult at 10,000
feet, and though not dangerous *per se*, planes rarely flew
there because of the possible damage to aircraft when
landing on hard, almost invisible sastrugi, and because it
was more expedient to parachute supplies to the Pole
from aircraft flying the round trip from Christchurch in
New Zealand.

There are no formalities in an Antarctic loo, and the
row of lavatory seats at McMurdo had no partitions. The
man next to me was an old polar hand who had wintered
over several times, and we were talking of this and that,
as one does when sharing a lavatory, when I moved
slightly – thank God, only slightly. As I squealed with
pain, the old polar hand knew just what had happened.

'For Chrissake don't budge.' He buttoned up his trousers
hurriedly. 'If you do, that goddam frozen metal will tear
off all the skin. Wait till I get the doc.'

I sat there, crouching motionless as a Buddha until the

McMurdo doctor arrived. 'No sweat,' he said cheerfully
and went to fetch a bowl of warm water.

He was carefully pouring it over my genitals when one
of the other journalists came into the toilets.

'What the hell are you doing?' he asked.

'I'm having warm water poured over my cock,' I hissed.
'I do it every day – greatest thrill there is.'

I came to no harm, though a warning notice was immediately posted in the loo. But I was a little sore, and Admiral
George Dufek, the US naval commander of all American
bases in Antarctica, felt that I needed a measure of med-
icinal Scotch in his plastic hut. Dufek was a real sailor,
grizzled, weatherbeaten, a salt-encrusted face, with the
discipline of a martinet cloaking a heart of gold.

'Always something going wrong in the Antarctic,' he
sighed. 'You'll be okay, but the damnedest thing has
happened at the Pole. One man has broken his denture
and can't chew his food properly. He's losing weight and
I'm worried.' Mechanics, he said, had tried to repair the
false teeth with aeroplane glue, but in vain. 'Even though
the weather's bad,' added George Dufek, 'I'll have to risk
flying a dentist up in a ski-plane.' (It is always 'up' to the
Pole.) I asked when he thought that might be.

'Four a.m. tomorrow,' replied Dufek.

'Mind if I bum a lift?'

He hesitated. I knew he was thinking of the other
journalists who were at McMurdo – two American agency
men and two likeable New Zealand boys anxious to report
on their hero Hillary, already on his way to the Pole by
tractor.

'If the weather gets better,' said Dufek, 'I was hoping I
might fly some of the press boys to the Pole for Christmas,
but we couldn't take more than two or three in the DC3,
so I planned to draw lots for places. If I let you go now,
it wouldn't be fair to the other boys if you were in the
Christmas draw. See my problem?'

On the assumption that tomorrow never comes, I said
I'd rather go right away.

'If you opt out of the Christmas draw, I see no reason why not,' said the Admiral.

And that is why I flew to the South Pole on Friday 13 November, and that is how chance took me on the first of three priceless bonus journeys of my life. None was dangerous, none involved problems of competition; each time I was enjoying isolated experiences in distant places that no money could buy.

The plane bumped over the rock-hard sastrugi and the four of us – dentist, pilot, a Navy lieutenant and myself – jumped out. The weather was closing in, but vague, shadowy, hooded figures groped their way towards us. The first figure materialised suddenly, like a man coming out of a thick fog, a shambling figure lonely against the white, with the unchanging hallmarks of Antarctica – goggles, rimed beard, fur-lined hood, enormous gloves dangling from tapes around the neck. Head down, shoulders hunched forward, he was unrecognisable: he could have been anybody from any time since Antarctic exploration started. This was timeless Antarctica; despite the technological advances of our world, man who strives to conquer that continent must still live largely in the world of yesterday.

Already the vague airstrip was almost invisible, though it was marked with a few strips of luminous scarlet 'Da-Glo', the modern version of the signals that Fred Ommanney used when he was lost in the Antarctic and held dead penguins upside down until their blood dripping against the white made a sign vivid enough to attract his rescuers.

I grabbed my survival kit and stumbled towards the group of black plastic huts linked by electric cables drooping with ice where eighteen men – nine scientists and their support party of nine American sailors – were spending a year without relief on ice half a mile thick, without ever seeing an animal, a blade of grass or any living creature other than their mates.

'Coffee coming up,' cried the chef in the galley as he cut a thick slice of snow from a large block and crammed it into a kettle.

We all took off parkas and pullovers and sat down at the dining table near the galley at one end of the long mess hall with its shining aluminium walls. This was the heart of the station, linked by 1,300 feet of tunnels to workshops, scientific labs, sleeping tents, tunnels used also for storing food and fuel (and a stock of 500 16-mm films). At the far end of the room was a projection screen which could be rolled down, a radiogram, and near it the 'post office', which consisted of a huge pile of parcels sent to the men by friends and relatives for the approaching Christmas.

The weather clamped down so badly that I spent several weeks at the Pole, trying to make myself as useful as possible and so pay for my keep – which included steaks almost every day, and never a steak weighing less than two pounds. (I could understand why the man needed his dentures.) Though it was possible to go out for short periods, the snow outside was so hard that it could not be used for water. This we obtained from a snow mine under one of the huts. By now the mine was 90 feet deep, with a constant temperature of around −50°C. We worked in shifts of fifteen minutes a day sawing blocks of snow to put in the snow melter above, for ironically water was our greatest problem and fire our greatest hazard.

Life was rough but wonderful. A fifteen-second shower once a week, next to the 'pee-hole', a deep pit into which the men urinated, and which by the time I arrived had a three-foot yellow stalagmite jutting up in it. The water froze almost as it touched it. Other refuse was buried in deep pits which were then snowed over. All refuse had to be carried by hand, and even used water could not be piped away, for it would freeze before it reached the pit.

Of course there was not much to *do* at the Pole. We had our movies, I wrote a great deal (in fact I wrote an article on Limoges porcelain, commissioned by the *Saturday Evening Post*, though I could not post it until I returned to New

Zealand). I also kept a diary which formed the basis of a book. But this was not a derring-do dateline story – not to me. It was a profound experience, and if anyone offered me a return trip I would go tomorrow.

As Christmas approached the signs of festivity increased, for though bad weather prevented us from leaving the Pole, Globemasters from Christchurch were parachuting down more and more letters and parcels, even a Christmas tree, together with a new supply of films, one of which was shown each evening in the mess hall. (The choice had to be made early as it took two hours to defrost a spool of film.)

But it was the ever-growing mound of parcels in the mess hall that excited everyone's attention, for Vern Houk, the young naval lieutenant in command of the base, had decreed that no parcels should be opened until Christmas morning. Of course no one could send *me* any parcels, yet I did not feel out of it. The experience, the accidental achievement of being there, the eerie sensation of utterly clean loneliness, the lifeless emptiness of the Polar Cap, stretching five hundred miles in every direction, reminded me of that great early explorer, Cherry-Garrard, who wrote that 'Polar exploration is at once the cleanest and most isolated way of having a bad time that has yet been devised'. Of course I missed Titina and the children, but I had been granted an experience that more than compensated for the lack of a new Charvet tie.

The morning of 25 December 'dawned' (after a night of blazing sunshine). I sat at the back of the mess hall while a sailor dressed as Father Christmas (Santa Claus to these Americans) called out the names and distributed the parcels, one or two at a time. There were none for me, of course – until suddenly my name *was* called. And then again – and again, and yet again. In all I had to walk up to the 'post office' near the radiogram eighteen times to collect parcels on which the name of the true recipient had been crossed out and mine substituted.

In deadly secrecy the previous night a plot had been

hatched. Each of the eighteen men at the Pole had contributed one *unopened* parcel as a gift to the lonely Limey house guest. It was the ultimate gesture of impulsive generosity, and I spent one of the happiest Christmas Days of my life.

I was still at the Pole when Edmund Hillary arrived on 4 January. The triumphant 'double' by the man who had climbed Everest caused terrific interest in England, particularly when details of his differences with Dr Fuchs were made public, and finally, when it was learned that, in order to reach the Pole, he had jettisoned all but fifteen gallons of his fuel on the last desperate stage.

Hillary's was a triumph of the first order, and Fleet Street made a meal of it. Alas for the *Daily Express*, they had been unable to get a reporter to the Pole, so I had the national newspaper field to myself. The rivalry between the *Mail* and *Express* was never greater than in those derring-do days, but on this occasion there was nothing the *Express* could do to catch up. Yet Hillary's triumph was the big news of the day and every newspaper in Britain splashed it across page 1. In the *Express* the headline roared:

HILLARY AT THE POLE

With a note of quiet superiority, the headline in the *Daily Mail* read simply:

BARBER LUNCHES WITH HILLARY

A paragraph in a newspaper led me to my second great bonus voyage, this time to the South Seas. It described how an American navy ship, sailing past a tiny uninhabited atoll, sent a helicopter ashore to gather fresh coconuts and when it landed, a man bounded on to the beach. He was a New Zealander called Tom Neale who had lived alone on the island for five years and refused a free passage back home. The atoll, called Suvarov, lay two hundred miles from the nearest small island, inhabited only by natives; it was seven hundred miles west of Tahiti. Tom Neale had no radio, no contact with the outside world apart from one or two pleasure yachts that called each year.

At the time England was going through a dreary period of strikes and frustration, and one newspaper had published a highly successful series on 'Male Slaves', telling of men born free but everywhere chained by family ties to desks and mortgages, while always dreaming of escape. Here was one man who had made his dream come true. All I had to do was learn whether he had found happiness, or whether his dream turned sour when realised.

The *Daily Mail*, bless its collective heart, jumped at the idea and I made first for Hawaii, to seek the advice of Dick Macmillan, who knows more about the South Seas (and how to get around them) than any man alive. Dick made a few calls, sent a few cables, and soon it transpired that only one vessel was available for charter. She lay at Pago Pago. I flew there immediately. (In my ignorance I imagined the islands would be full of old yachts ready for work, but obviously I had been reading too much Maugham.)

Pago Pago (pronounced *Pango Pango*) had not changed since Maugham conceived Sadie Thompson in the Rain-maker Hotel, facing the sea on Broad Road by the edge of the bay, somehow at odds with the trim bungalows of the American officials. True to Maugham's story it hardly stopped raining while I was there. If the sun did come out, then I could watch a grey cloud over the rain forest in the mountains behind drift slowly towards the town; once it arrived, the water came down in sheets. There was only one thing to do – forget it, like the brown Samoans, their dark curly hair sometimes dyed white with lime, who strode through the rain not so much with resolution or resignation but as though it just wasn't there.

I was in Maugham country all right, for by chance the boat I chartered, the *Manua Tele*, was the same one in which Maugham travelled from Pago Pago to Apia in 1916 after spending a week with the characters who later came to life in 'Rain'. He described the vessel then as 'a schooner of seventy tons with paraffin auxilliary . . . a bedraggled craft, painted white long ago and now dirty, dingy and mottled'. As when Maugham sailed on her, we carried a captain, two engineers, and half a dozen kanakas, who spent the last morning bringing fresh supplies aboard in baskets woven out of green banana leaves. Since I was chartering, I had the 'best' cabin – two berths, but the ceiling not quite high enough for me to stand upright. Maugham did not mention that the *Manua Tele* was infested with cockroaches and rats. However, since she was the only boat large enough to make the four-day journey to Suvarov, I had no option but to take her.

For four days (at £150 a day) the *Manua Tele* wallowed across the Pacific, fighting the trade winds, rolling, bucking, heaving, until at dawn on the fifth day we sighted Suvarov – very low, the skyline fringed with bending palms behind a blinding white beach and the limpid green water inside the snarling breakers of the reef.

While I was breakfasting on deck off fried bananas, greasy bacon and warm beer (the fridge had broken down), the island came into finer focus; a dot of land in the immensity of the Pacific, a few acres of lush green vegetation, fenced in by a million year's growth of coral. It represented man's most elusive and tantalising dream – the dream of escape from the dull grind of a despised job, from the bickering and mockery of a bitter life, from what is often a strangling captivity; escape from all that makes life so difficult: working to pay taxes that are frittered away on obsolescent armaments by pompous politicians; fog, sleet and snow; strikes, traffic jams, neighbours.

As we dropped anchor in the lagoon, I saw a spurt of movement near the beach. At first I thought it was an animal, but it was a man, running out of the palm grove on to the beach, flashing a mirror into the sun to attract our attention. He had a small boat, and was soon sailing across the lagoon to meet us. Half an hour later Tom Neale was aboard, sipping warm beer.

On the journey from Pago I had often wondered what my first words would be when I met this modern Robinson Crusoe. (I couldn't say 'Mr·Neale, I presume!') But what I could never have guessed was *his* first extraordinary question after we had exchanged greetings. As he opened his second can of beer, he asked, 'Tell me something – did that photographer fella ever marry Princess Margaret?'

The island on which Tom had lived for five years was half a mile long, barely three hundred yards across, yet its position is marked on every good atlas because the tiny chunk of coral lies inside a vicious reef with a circumference of fifty miles or more which is known as a danger to shipping. It had been inhabited only once in its existence, during World War Two when a hut and water tanks were built to house a party of plane-spotters with a wireless. During the war, when Tom was a ship's engineer, he had called at Suvarov with stores. He fell in love with the island and that is why at the age of fifty-eight he returned, inheriting the hut and water tanks.

For companions he had two cats, and the population of a chicken run at the bottom of a tidy, productive garden. In one of the hut's three rooms was his office, a table covered with brown paper, a home-made chair, a hurricane lamp, a 400-day clock, an elementary first-aid box and on the wall, in his careful handwriting, a list of ships that had called – six in five years.

Next to the office was his bedroom, a home-made wooden frame for a bed and on it a palliasse, a pillow, and a brightly coloured lava-lava, the South Seas sarong, to make sure he didn't catch a chill at night. In his kitchen – the third room – Tom had used some old wire netting which he had found on the island to build a meat safe for the fowl he killed and in this he put some fresh bread I brought him, the first he'd had in two years, some

butter and a four-pound joint of beef. Ranging the walls
were pots and pans, two black kettles, a dishcloth and his
razor. 'I shave every Wednesday and Sunday,' said Tom,
'and I make a blade last three months by sharpening it on
the inside of a wet glass.'

Outside Tom had built a cookhouse where he cooked
the fish he speared each day, and breadfruit, coconut
scones, chickens, eggs or the produce of his garden –
bananas, sweet potatoes, papaw and a luscious vine called
Indian spinach. Down on the beach, under the shade of
fronded palms, he had built a small lean-to shack, roofed
with attap, which he called his summer house, and he spent
the last beautiful moments of dusk there each evening.
He had hacked a path back to the main hut,
and another one to a small beach on the other side
of the island – three hundred yards away. It was idyllic.
There were few flies, no mosquitoes, no snakes or
bugs, just the murmur of gentle waves and a whispering
wind.

'I've never been in better health,' he said, and he certainly looked in fine condition for a man in his sixties,
seven hundred miles from the nearest doctor. His thin
body was mahogany stained, his eyes clear, though never
still, and set deep in a map of tiny wrinkles. He never
suffered from toothache, because before setting out for
the island he had had all his teeth extracted. He cut his
greying hair with the aid of an old mirror.

It was hard work that helped to keep him fit. 'There's
always something to be done,' he explained. 'The path to
the hut has to be trimmed twice a week or you wouldn't
be able to walk through it. Sometimes if I get a touch of
fever and lay off for a few days, I have to work twelve
hours a day to get things back to normal.'

In the South Seas the products of nature grow at a
remorseless rate, while the products of man disintegrate
with equal swiftness. Over the beach hut grew a huge mau
tree, gnarled, twisting branches almost covering the roof.
Tom had planted a sapling there only five years previously.

The garden could become a tangle in a few days, while the attap roof could start to let in water. In the tropics there is no peace for the blessed.

Luckily Tom was a practical man as well as a dreamer; otherwise he could never have stuck it out. And, a quality doubtless accentuated by his lonely life, he was finicky, as I discovered when he brewed a cup of tea from the supplies I brought him. As he rinsed the old teapot round and round with boiling water he said, 'I can't *stand* tea from a cold pot.'

It took time before I could discover what had impelled Tom to come here. He was not shy – far from it, he never stopped talking – and he was no crank. I remember the scene when I first asked him: the black, beautiful night, the hurricane lamp between us, Tom's brown face half lit, two cups and the empty pot on the home-made beach table, one of the cats sitting upright, the palms whispering, the lights of the *Manua Tele* blinking in the bay.

'I've always wanted to live in a place on my own as an experiment,' he said finally. 'I always felt I could do it. I always knew inside myself that I wouldn't feel lonely and it turned out that way. There's nothing more to it really. I've never been lonely on Suvarov – well, hardly ever. The only time I got a bit fed up was when I ran out of tobacco. That made me feel moody; I didn't eat the same, I didn't work the same. It took me two months to get over it.

'Of course,' he went on, 'people think you just decide one day and up anchor the next. That's nonsense. I've been sailing round the islands all my life. The real truth is that you don't make decisions like this all at once. I'd been growing towards the idea for thirty years. But don't get me wrong. I'm no hermit. And I'm not trying to evade responsibilities, because I don't have any. I suppose really, honestly, I don't quite know why I did come here in the first place.'

I would have stayed a month, had it not been for the cost of the charter. When the time came to leave, I said to Tom, almost casually, 'You could write a wonderful book about your island. If you ever leave it, and if you ever need any help putting your diaries in order, let me know. I'll do anything I can.' I never thought, as we sailed away, that one day Tom Neale would give me the chance to change *my* life, and travel again when I thought that my wandering days were over.

Chance took me to Suvarov and it was chance that took me on my third journey to distant places, this time to the remote mountainous country of Hunza, north of Pakistan, and less than twenty miles from the Sinkiang border. Locked in by snow-capped peaks, there is only one narrow, ninety-mile mountain ledge along which one can reach Hunza, where eighteen thousand people and their king, called the Mir, live in perfect tranquillity without money, police, cars, telephones, hotels, soldiers.

I was having a drink in Paris with Aly Khan who announced that he had to leave early to receive the Mir of Hunza, whose Moslem people were followers of the Aga Khan. I had only heard vaguely of Hunza as the country which James Hilton is supposed to have had in mind when creating Shangri-La. Aly arranged for me to meet the Mir.

He was a charming, portly, affable man who spoke excellent English, and obviously thoroughly enjoyed his occasional excursions to Europe, a holiday away from the chores of being absolute monarch of the internal affairs of his country (the external affairs being looked after by Pakistan in those days).

'But you must come and visit us – please do, stay with me in the palace,' he insisted, and though visitors were not really welcome – for one thing there was no hotel where they could stay – I remembered my father once advising me never to refuse an offer because one might not be asked a second time. 'I'd love to,' I said, speaking for the *Daily Mail* (and convinced they would foot the bill).

It was as easy as that. After the necessary paper work I set off for Rawalpindi, and from there flew in a Pakistan Army plane to Gilgit, a town not served by commercial airlines, possibly because there were no weather aids, and the only route lies between mountains that almost brushed our wings. I spent the night at Gilgit with the District Officer and the following morning set off in a jeep along the High Pass, very much like the path along which Ronald Colman left Shangri-La, a narrow, flinty ledge, most of it cut into the precipitous slopes of mountains; at times the pass rose to fifteen thousand feet, and I hardly dared to look down the sheer drops of up to six thousand feet, for though wide enough for a jeep, it could not take a Land Rover, and was so narrow that at times we had to stop the jeep to let a pedestrian squeeze past.

Finally we turned the last corner, and there in front of us lay Hunza – terraced green fields hemmed in by white peaks and far below, the grey glacial waters of the Hunza River, heartbeat of the country. It really *was* like Shangri-La, with the Mir's palace on a bluff overlooking the fields and river below, just like the ornate palace in *Lost Horizon*, though the Mir's was constructed of wood and looked more like a Swiss chalet, with a sign over the portico reading 'Welcome'.

'I hope the journey was worth it.' The Mir took my arm and led me in for luncheon – one of the most curious meals I have ever eaten.

'We don't drink a great deal,' said the Mir, 'but in your honour . . .' The white aperitif tasted delicious, almost like a vermouth. It was made of apricots.

'Have a chip.' The Mir produced some crisps – made from dried, thinly-shaven apricots. The glistening silver salver caught my attention. 'It *does* shine well,' agreed the Mir. 'I suppose you know that if you rub an old penny or piece of silver with the sauce your prime minister is so fond of, you can make it shine like new. Well,' – with an apologetic chuckle – 'we call ours AS sauce – for apricot – and I can tell you, it cleans metal ten times better than HP.'

We started with apricot soup, flavoured with herbs, followed by a salad which included apricots as well as radishes, sliced because in Hunza radishes grow to a length of two feet; this was followed by a kind of hamburger of apricots mixed with wheat. We drank apricot wine and ended with apricot brandy – almost too banal, this echo from my own world.

The only other drink was water, but when my glass arrived it contained a dirty grey sludge, so I waited for this to settle before taking a polite sip. 'No, no!' cried the Mir. 'You are missing the best part.' Giving my glass a vigorous stir, he said, 'Now it's ready to drink!' It was glacial water, and had been drunk like this, with all its valuable mineral deposits, for two thousand years, since the day when three soldiers from the armies of Alexander the Great stumbled on the hidden valley, promptly deserted and took Persian wives, who bore the first dark-skinned, fair-haired Hunzakuts.

Lunch over, the Mir offered to show me around; and I soon discovered that the apricots and the glacial water were far more fascinating than the brilliant scenery, for they were largely responsible for a precious secret for which man has been searching in vain since the dawn of time – the secret of long life.

The Mir introduced me to one man of a hundred and eighteen who had just returned from a five-mile walk. I went to the christening of a newborn son while his father of eighty-nine stood by chuckling. Men of eighty looked forty. Disease seemed to be unknown. Children never caught measles or mumps. There had never been a recorded case of cancer, heart disease or tuberculosis.

'There's the secret.' The Mir pointed to the mountains that isolate Hunza. 'They're rich in minerals. The glacial waters gather them as they tumble towards the valley, so that by the time we get a glass of water here, it has a thick sediment. Now you understand why I asked you to drink it.'

The people of Hunza irrigate their land with this water, so that it leaves a thick silt of mineral deposit which impregnates their fruit and vegetables with a magic potion beyond price – so precious that no fruit is ever peeled, and most vegetables are eaten raw. And there are three crops a year, largely of the staple food of apricots, all grown in soil that has never known a chemical fertiliser.

The 'rules' for longevity included, I discovered, *always* drinking the water in which the food has been cooked. And though there are plenty of cows, the people rarely drink milk, but make it into yoghurt or a hard spicy cheese. They thresh their wheat freshly every day. In fact in a country which does not have any money and where every man is his own master, the miller is one of the few men with a regular job because it is more intelligent for one man to thresh wheat for several families than for each man to do it separately. He is paid in the only way possible – with free meals from the families he helps.

The secret of long life in Hunza must go deeper than diet. Man cannot live on bread alone, even if the wheat is grown in mineral silt. And I am sure that I found in Hunza the other half of the secret, for the country possesses one priceless gift, that of serenity. There are no *vices* in Hunza – no jealousy, no envy, no avarice, since the root of all evil does not exist in a self-sufficient country. The people of Hunza need nothing really from the outside world except perhaps kerosene and matches, which they get by carrying baskets of fruit over the High Pass and bartering them in Gilgit.

I have never seen such absence of stress, of even the simplest frustrations. No traffic jams because there is no traffic. The children cannot play cops and robbers because they have no idea what cops and robbers are.

The Hunza philosophy – its good luck, if you like – was summed up by the Mir (who owns the only jeep in town). This genial father-figure told me, 'Nothing can hurt my people because they don't *know* what hurts you people of the outside world. We are blessed with what I call inno-cence through ignorance.'

15

LUNCHEON IS SERVED

CERTAIN OF THE natives in Malaya were not very friendly in the fifties, but I did revenge myself on one who displeased the British Raj. I ate him.

The country was in the grip of the 'Emergency', a vicious war that lasted twelve years, in which thousands of Chinese Communists tortured and murdered rubber planters and tin miners and their families, together with law-abiding 'running dogs', the name contemptuously bestowed on the locals whose crime was daring to help the British.

As a war correspondent, I went on one patrol with six young conscripts and a second lieutenant who were attempting to track down a hidden Communist camp deep in the jungle. We were accompanied by two Dyak headhunters, presumably unemployed, who were highly skilled jungle trackers, and could kill instantly with poisonous darts which they aimed unerringly through long blowpipes. It was a wretched week, fascinating only in retrospect. At times we trudged or slithered waist deep in swamp. We could not cook, smoke, even wash with soap because of the jungle fighters' highly developed sense of smell.

Had I been on pleasure bent, carefully protected against a malevolent nature by guides whose task was to cosset me, the experience would have been wonderful; instead I was hiding in a jungle that was a world of its own with hissing rains, imprisoned by tall straight trees pointing upwards for a hundred feet or more or branching out in tufts of fat green leaves or flowers, or with the twisting root-branches of the mangrove swamp hanging like the rigging of a forlorn shipwreck. Around us the rain forest was alive with chattering monkeys, squeaking parrots, with snakes slithering along the dead leaves, with fat leeches waiting patiently on saplings or ferns for someone to brush against them. And above all else, there was the hum of never-absent mosquitoes.

After nearly a week we found the Chinese camp, guarded by a sentry. Without a sound one of the Dyaks killed him with a dart from his blowpipe. We cut off the man's hands and head for identification (it is too hot in Malaya to carry a whole body back to base), and razed the camp, after capturing those who did not have time to flee.

At last all need for secrecy was over. To celebrate we lit our first fire for a week; I brushed my teeth and bathed in a stream, then we prepared to heat up some K rations; the Dyaks offered to lope into the nearest village to find fresh food. No questions were asked when they returned with a haversack filled with thick, juicy steaks. Never did a tournedos taste better.

The meal over, discipline was restored and a burial party was ordered to dispose of the Communist sentry's body. Only then was it discovered that a large part of his thigh – large enough to provide several steaks – was missing. To the Dyaks it must have seemed like home from home. Several of the youngsters were sick, but to be truthful, the meat seemed no better or worse than many steaks I have eaten in different parts of the world; a little sweet perhaps, but no more so than the horsemeat occasionally dished up by Marie-Lou in the bistro next to the *Continental Daily Mail* in Paris.

Some years later I casually mentioned this incident in a BBC travel talk, and the following Sunday I went to 11 Downing Street for a pre-lunch drink with brother Tony. I cannot remember which of us opened the *Sunday Express* first, but there was no disguising the unequivocal headline:

DID YOU KNOW
THE CHANCELLOR'S
BROTHER IS A
CANNIBAL?

When I visited Hunza, I had been intrigued by the Mir's cocktail snacks made of apricots, but I had to wait many years before being offered an equally unusual titbit. The dish was served by Olga Deterding, eccentric (to say the least) heiress to several million pounds, who had at one time left all that her world represented to live and work for several years with Albert Schweitzer in the Congo.

I first met Olga in 1953, when I decided to write a column about New Year's Eve in St Moritz, and had installed myself in the Palace Hotel. Olga was there, sporting a pair of highly attractive pink *après-ski* pants, and I described how snugly they fitted her posterior. In the first edition of the *Daily Mail* my words were somehow scrambled, and passing reference made to Miss Deterding's 'pink bottom'. We have been firm friends ever since. We met again when she gave a party to launch Jonothan Routh's 'Queen Victoria' paintings.

By then, Olga had moved into a two-storey penthouse in Clarges Street, with a magnificent view over Green Park. The ceiling between the two floors had been pierced to accommodate a spiral staircase. The room was crowded with celebrities. Two grave butlers in full fig served magnums of Krug. Two trimly-aproned maids appeared with trays of hot snacks.

'You'll *adore* them,' said Olga. 'I discovered them the other day in a supermarket – quite by chance.' As I hesitated, she teased me, 'Oh come on, Noel – don't be such a fuddy-duddy. You of all people can't be scared of trying something new for a change. I've just *discovered* them.'

I must say her confidence was justified, even though it was the first time I had ever drunk Krug with fish fingers.

I have eaten foods from virtually every country, but I still love my English food, and I think many Britons do our country a disservice by continually denigrating home cooking. No doubt, if you want to eat cheaply you get better value for money in a small French bistro or an

Italian trattoria than in an English 'caff'. No doubt that in restaurant after restaurant in Britain, in home after home, you will be served cabbage swimming in water. Yet we have dishes fit for a king in Britain, though because we refuse to admit it to foreigners, no one in Europe will believe it, least of all the French.

After a wonderful dinner once at the Pyramide in Vienne, I drank a Napoleon brandy with the redoubtable Monsieur Point himself, and the talk turned to English food. I enthused on some of our remarkable dishes that were virtually unknown to foreigners. The greatest chef in all France seemed doubtful but, trying to show he was unbiased, said, '*Mais oui, cher monsieur.* There is nothing wrong with English food. All you have to do is eat breakfast three times a day.'

Because of our inferiority complex about our food, the British tend to take it out on the Americans, with sweeping generalisations (mostly by those who have never visited America) about tasteless, over-frozen, canned American food. Yet real American food is superb. During the two years I lived in San Francisco, I grew to love it. Of course in restaurants one has to read warily between the lines of what Kenneth Allsop called 'the poetry of the American menu'. It can be disheartening to be enticed by an item reading:

Try our exotic, peach-fed product of
Arkansas, served to your special requirements,
garnished with the choicest fruit of sun-drenched
Hawaii, and nestling on a crisp, green bed of
lettuce

– only to find that you have ordered a gammon rasher with pineapple.

The poetry of the menu is often changed radically by the waitresses, especially in those places where orders are shouted across the room to the chef at a long bar. When I was once working a night shift in San Francisco, I always had supper at three o'clock in the morning, always served by the same cheerful waitress called Dolly, in the inevitable waitress's white shoes, at the same table in a Sutter Street all-night restaurant. One night I was stricken with agonising toothache. Determined to uphold the 'the show must go on' tradition, I reached the office by midnight, and worked without much enthusiasm until it was time to visit my usual restaurant. When I refused all solid food, a sympathetic Dolly pointed to an item on the menu:

> Tender cubes of fluffy home-baked bread
> floating gently in a crock of rich, creamy
> dairy produce straight from our own farms.

I was smart enough to know bread and milk when I saw it, and of course it was just what I wanted. I was a little disconcerted though, and felt a little older, when Dolly, in stentorian voice, shouted across the room, 'One portion of graveyard stew!'

Sometimes the circumstances surrounding an invitation are so curious that one forgets what is on the menu, and this certainly happened when I dined *à deux* with General Jean de Lattre de Tassigny, commander-in-chief of the French forces in Indo-China before the Vietnam war of course. A man who was thoroughly disliked by most Allied generals, de Lattre was shunted off to Indo-China after Eisenhower refused point-blank to have him anywhere near his post-war headquarters in Paris. As one of Ike's aides told me, 'He's an awkward bugger.' Uncharitable people summed him up by using even stronger language. De Lattre was not a pleasant man.

Like many Frenchmen he could never forget the shame of their abject defeat by the Germans; but even worse, he could never forgive the British for *not* having lost it, nor the Americans for having won it.

As a result he took a twisted delight in scoring off people

in no position to answer back. He was, however, extremely well informed on South-East Asia, and that was why I dined with him.

The invitation came originally when I was invited to a luncheon for eight at the Ritz in Paris, arranged by Harold King, the brilliant head of Reuters there, and one of the few Englishmen de Gaulle called '*mon ami*'. I was seated next to de Lattre and said to him, in much the same way as I had once asked Churchill to give me the benefit of his advice, 'I only wish I could dine alone with you, *mon général*, and we could have a real talk about what's happening in South-East Asia.'

'Nothing simpler, my dear Barber,' he replied. 'Come and dine with me on Saturday. Just the two of us. Black tie.'

'Of course,' I murmured.

For fully half a minute de Lattre weighed up how long I could keep my cool, before adding smoothly, 'I should have mentioned – Saigon, of course.'

'Naturally,' I replied as though the prospect of dinner in any other city was unthinkable. 'Eight o'clock?'

Saigon is 7,130 miles from Paris. On Wednesday I received my movement orders from the French Air Force, and that night I telephoned New York and arranged a commission for a 5,000-word article on South-East Asia from an editor who was delighted that no expenses would be involved. Late on Thursday I flew out of Paris, arriving in Saigon on Saturday afternoon. At the one and only Continental, I had a shower, shave and snooze, before changing into my tropical dinner jacket, and charging my tape recorder.

'So glad you could come,' said de Lattre, to whom I had given my word that the conversation I taped would never be attributed to him. We dined, we drank, while I kept my eye on the clock, for an Air Force transport was leaving around midnight, and I could not afford to miss it because I had an important engagement in Paris the following week. After an excellent meal, topped off with a large brandy, I apologised, 'I'm afraid, sir, I really *must* be getting home.'

The next day I was back in Paris. Within a week I had typed out and rewritten de Lattre's masterly summing-up – and dire prophecies – of South-East Asia. Within a month I received $1,000 for the article – all this and dinner too.

De Lattre de Tassigny had been a considerate host on that occasion, but I had much more fun when supping, quite by chance, in the company of Porfirio Rubirosa, one of the most elegant members of his jet-set era and (apparently) lover extraordinary, with a horizontal stamina said to equal that of Aly Khan, at whose house we met. At the last moment my partner had been taken ill. She had insisted – really, rather against my will – that I borrow her beautiful gold Fabergé cigarette case.

It was a large supper party and Rubirosa and I, who had not been introduced, started desultory conversation while helping ourselves to the cold buffet. I had no partner to look after and Rubirosa seemed bored.

'Damn!' he said. 'I've run out of cigarettes.'

I offered him mine, nestling snugly in their gold case. As he took one, he looked at me strangely, and said, 'Who are you?'

My first thought was not very charitable, but in the event I told him my name, at which he persisted, 'Can I have a look at that case? Where did you get it?'

I began to visualise a tortured history of fences and French *flics*, but then he suddenly smiled and said, very politely, 'Forgive me, please – but it was the shock of seeing that case again. I'm sure it once belonged to me. There can't be two like it.'

He was examining the case and then, with an almost dreamy look, he explained, 'I *gave* that cigarette case to a really stunning girl one Christmas. I remember, it was in New York, at a large party given by Igor Cassini – you know, the American columnist who wrote under the name of Cholly Knickerbocker.'

I nodded. Rubirosa continued, 'This beautiful girl had just arrived from Europe, and there was a Christmas tree in the corner. She didn't have a single present hanging on it. I was so touched that I went into the next room, took out my case – *this* case, I'm sure – and wrapped it up, put her name on it, and hung it on the tree. I wonder where she is today.' He searched his memory, and suddenly her name came to him. 'I wonder if she ever married.'

'Yes, she did,' I replied. 'I know the name.'

'I wonder why she had to sell the case. Sad, really – she seemed to love it so much. I hope she married well.'

'Not *very* well,' I replied. 'She's my wife.'

Rubirosa had been an amusing dinner companion, but a meal with Somerset Maugham could be hazardous. I was always free to invite myself to the Villa Mauresque, and did so when brother Ken accompanied me on an assignment in the South of France. Ken, who started out cashing cheques behind the grille of a bank and finally became one of its highest executives, has a profound knowledge of literature, art and music and I knew he would be delighted to meet the master; but I warned him that Maugham's temper was unpredictable.

The admirable Alan Searle was the fourth at table, and from the start of a desultory lunch it was evident that Willie was in a filthy mood. He had long since refined the art of showing the extent of his boredom by the use of the most exquisite politeness, and by the time we had reached the avocado ice cream nobody was saying much. Then my brother, seeking to make conversation, asked, 'Are you doing much travelling these days, Mr Maugham?'

'Well yes, I *am*.' Every word, uttered in his thin, piping voice, seemed to be dragged out painfully. 'Alan and I are off next to Genoa.'

'By car, I suppose?'

'Exactly.' Willie could even make a nod of assent look agonised, as though appalled at having to explain to people that nobody ever travelled to Genoa except by car.

'Should be fun,' I chimed in.

'And when are you going?' Ken asked innocently.

'Actually, Mr Barber,' – Willie studied his watch osten-
tatiously – 'precisely two minutes after you leave.'

16

NATURAL BREAK

WHEN I REGAINED consciousness, my body twisted and trapped under the smashed steering wheel, the first thing I saw on the deserted road was a car completely sliced in two. To the left two bodies slumped over the front seats. To the right, several yards away, two more bodies lay in grotesque positions on the rear seat.

It was 11 a.m. on Friday, 5 July 1960 – barely six months after we had sold our farm on Lake Geneva and decided that, after all, life would be more fun in good old England, even with taxes. I was owed six weeks' leave, so we borrowed a flat in Monte Carlo, and at 9 a.m. on that Friday I had landed at Le Touquet after flying the Channel from Lydd with my car, a Super Snipe. Fortified by an espresso and a croissant at the Lido, Le Touquet's spotless airport restaurant, I headed south. The car was loaded with personal belongings, including linen, needed for the holiday. Titina and the children planned to fly directly to Nice where I would pick them up.

North of Beauvais, bowling along in a blinding rainstorm, I approached a long, narrow incline. Half-way up I saw through the wipers a Citroën tear over the brow, skid, and slither towards me sideways on, gathering speed with every yard. I wrenched the wheel hard right towards the grass verge.

The fact that I was in a car with a right-hand drive saved my life, for the Citroën hit me on the left-hand front corner with such force that the dashboard penetrated the left front seat and protruded into the back of the car. But the French car had slewed round so badly that it took the impact at a point between its front and rear doors; since the Citroën has a front-wheel drive it has no chassis in our sense of the word.

The visual shock when I came to was followed instantly by a terrible fear that it was all my fault. I remember nothing until I woke in a village hospital for old people, where I had been dumped in the corner of a ward for senile men. In a daze, I saw them lined up in a row by a nurse while they tried to pass water into bottles. In the same daze I could hear words like, 'English . . . Murderer . . . Car crash . . .'

I managed to ask a nurse to phone Robin Smyth, then chief of the *Daily Mail* Paris bureau, and an old friend. When he arrived a couple of hours later he telephoned Titina, refraining from reading to her the macabre headline in one French evening newspaper:

BRITISH MOTORIST MURDERS FOUR

Robin had driven out in an ambulance and we set off for Paris, where French doctors were waiting for me in a hospital. One stretched out my left leg which seemed to be badly twisted. Then they started stitching up my head, for the force of the impact had split open a great deal of scar tissue, a legacy from the fifty-two stitches needed after being shot in the head in Budapest.

Local anaesthetics dulled the pain, but if only the French were not such purists! All I wanted was to *live*, or to be left alone, or even as a last resort, to die. The question of being slightly disfigured by a couple of cuts seemed unimportant. The doctors had other ideas. After putting fifteen stitches in my head, they came to a hefty cut that sliced through my left eyebrow. I asked feebly if the cut was still bleeding. No, it wasn't. I suggested in French, 'To hell with it, just shove a bit of plaster on.'

'Mais, ce n'est pas esthétique,' said one doctor in a shocked voice.

'I do think we could manage with just two stitches,' said the other.

'C'est impossible!' cried the first. 'We need four or five

at least to make sure the scar never shows. I will not be
associated with any slapdash methods.' And damn it, he
almost threatened to down tools and strike over my demar-
cation line.

I do not know how many stitches they settled for, but I
have to admit that the scar is only superficial. Then the
doctors came to my right knee, which felt no worse than
it had done when as a boy I fell off a galloping horse and
grazed a leg.

'You play ze sport?' asked the eager beaver with a glint
in his eyes. I admitted to this failing. 'Yes, ze British, of
course. *Vive le sport*! Then, monsieur, if you wear shorts,
your knee must be made pretty.'

The demonstration of needlework lasted so long that it
was some time before I realised that the stitches were the
least of my worries. My right arm hurt violently. So did
my left foot. Two or three fingers seemed numb. And my
mouth seemed curious, filled with something. When I
moved my tongue to the left, I realised that several teeth
were hanging, half out of their sockets. As for my left thigh
– that was hell.

'*Oui, je comprends, monsieur,*' said the doctor, '*attendez
quelques minutes, s'il vous plaît.*'

Finally they left. Two more doctors arrived. A portable
X-ray showed that my left thigh was broken in five places,
so they decided to put it into traction. For this they had to
drill a hole through the shin bone and insert a steel pin
protruding on either side of the leg so that they could
attach cords to it and slowly, with weights over the end of
the bed, straighten and pull out my leg which had shortened
by two inches.

It was a long job, but, as they explained apologetically,
I was too weak to be given a general anaesthetic. With this
I could only agree. I felt terrible. I felt even worse when
one doctor produced a kind of drill with a small wheel
and a handle on the side to turn it. Having selected the
appropriate target area, he started turning, very, very
slowly.

A couple of hours later, when they had finished, I tried
to point to my teeth; I complained about my feet and my
fingers. My right wrist was hurting. But by now it was
getting late and someone gave me a jab.

All this was but a prelude to the macabre scene that
followed after Titina's arrival. I was still feeling out of
sorts, and when I looked at myself in the mirror which
Titina placed before me, I found that every inch of my
body was purple. In an effort to cheer me up, since it was
obvious that I was not going to die, Titina and one nurse
held mirrors so that I could see the middle portion of my
body. My testicles were the size of grapefruit.

Within a few days two specialists arrived. They examined
my left leg gravely, with much head-shaking, and muttered
darkly. One seemed to be keen on hunting for I heard him
say, *'Mais jeudi, c'est pas possible. N'oubliez pas j'ai un
rendezvous à la chasse!'*

There was clearly a problem there. While I looked
on half doped (and frankly not caring very much what
happened), they each took out their pocket diaries and
consulted them. Obviously, they were discussing dates
(hopefully the day when I could be flown home) and there
was a great deal of head-shaking and pursed lips and
spectacle-polishing. In the midst of this Titina poked her
head round the door. The horrified doctors tried to shoo
her out. Titina smiled and pushed her way in.

I was astounded to see her, for we had agreed that she
should return to London for three or four days, settle the
children, deal with the outstanding problems, and return.
But she had decided to stay a day longer, saying merely,
'I had a feeling that you might need me.'

With this she pleasantly wished the doctors good morning and inquired as to the state of my health.

'He is very lucky,' said one gloomily.

'When can we get him back to England?' asked Titina.

'Mais, madame!' He was horrified. 'Your husband is
very ill. Not for weeks, perhaps months. We have to
operate.'

I chimed in hopefully, 'My teeth?' for they were still dangling like pendants.

The nurse chimed in, 'These are two of the greatest orthopaedic surgeons in France, madame.'

Titina chimed in, 'Operate?'

'Mais oui,' said one specialist. 'The day after tomorrow. I'm sorry, madame, but we have to amputate.'

'Over my dead body!' blurted out Titina.

With pursed lips the specialist retorted, 'Madame, we do not usually discuss details of this sort with ladies.' Patiently he explained that at my advanced age there was little hope of my muscles ever holding the leg together again, and as for the thigh itself, the surgeon added a sentence I still remember. *'C'est un mosaïque,'* he declared.

Titina stormed out to the nearest telephone, and phoned Esmond (after all he *had* been best man at our wedding). He went into action immediately. That afternoon Bill Hardcastle, then editor of the *Daily Mail*, arrived to throw his considerable weight around. The operation was postponed. And a week later, against the dire warnings of the French, I was put in plaster from head to toe, flown to Gatwick in a chartered plane, whisked through customs to an ambulance which I commanded to stop at the nearest pub for a pint of English bitter (very difficult to drink lying flat on one's back), and then sped off to the London Clinic where David Trevor, one of the greatest geniuses in the bone business, examined me.

After discovering that the French had omitted to examine my right wrist which was fractured, my left foot which was broken and two fingers which were also broken, he said, 'You have a chance. Because you've played sports all your life you're in much better condition than the average man of your age. But it's a gamble, only a fifty-fifty chance that we can save the leg. The only thing is – I'll have to set the bone and put you in traction and then I won't be able to tell you anything for sixteen weeks. I won't even be able to examine the leg, except for X-rays. Can you wait?'

It took a long time, but a year later I threw my crutches away, and two years later I was back in France, playing singles for the British International Club Veterans' team against Jean Borotra, a feat that would have been extremely difficult had Titina not remained an extra day in Paris.

Sometimes when I think about God, the mysterious forces of which we are so ignorant, the hereafter – whether it is all real or just the mumbo-jumbo of the ouija-board – I think of one instance related to my car crash.

When in 1942 brother Tony baled out of his Spitfire over the Channel and was missing for three months, I was A/C2 Barber, the lowest form of human life in the RAF, and I waited one evening until the Nissen hut was empty, then knelt and prayed for Tony's safety. I was too selfish a bastard to offer my life for his, but I did pray, 'If You will bring him back to us, please take one of my legs in exchange.'

Better than nothing, and damn it, the very next evening Lord Haw-Haw broadcast Tony's name in a list of prisoners-of-war. Was 11 a.m. on that fateful Friday so many years later the moment chosen to make good the promissory note? Was it my appointment in Samarra? And if so, did He say in effect, 'Barber is a sonofabitch and he'll certainly never make a saint, but there are so many child-beaters around whose arms I haven't had time to chop off, that maybe we'll give the old ram another break.'

Humbly I offer my gratitude, using the phrase of a young Catholic priest who holds his God in awe when in church, but once outside tends, like many a fervent Catholic, to regard Him as a good pal, a wise friend. I still play tennis with the good father at Queen's every Saturday, and I echo now the phrase he mutters every time he serves an ace:

'Thanks, Top Man.'

I was often in pain when lying in the London Clinic, for I

had to remain in one position for nearly five months, but I was never afraid as I had been in France, for there I faced the terrors of the unknown – helpless in the hands of men I instinctively distrusted, but whose decisions I was too weak to contest.

Fear evaporates with confidence. I was not afraid when I was shot in Budapest in 1956, because the doctor who clamped my wrists to the operating table to prevent me jerking my arms while putting fifty-two stitches in my head without any anaesthetic exuded calm. Almost casually he remarked, 'You're no worse off than half the motorists we treat every week-end.'

I was far more terrified when I had toothache in Barbados, after jabbing my gum with a fork. Though the wound was superficial my face the next morning was like a pumpkin, and I have lived long enough in the tropics to know that one can be poisoned, die and be buried in the space of a few hours unless one is careful. I needed treatment quickly, but it was a Sunday and only one dentist was working.

It was very hot as I walked across the padang to his surgery. Once inside I discovered that he was attending several patients at the same time, having divided his surgery with muslin curtains into sections; from them I heard arguing, moaning, even screaming.

The dentist was very black. I mention this with no disrespect, but rather because I have always had an uneasy feeling that a medical diploma in some countries is not the result of such meritorious and prolonged study as in Europe and America; an opinion held ever since I saw a sign outside a Chinese dental surgery in Singapore which read:

ALL DENTAL WORK
UNDERTAKEN

ARTIFICIAL EYES
ALSO FIXED

After the dentist had darted from one section to another, drilling a bit here, hacking a little there, it was my turn. He took one look at my face and announced flatly, 'It's an abscess all right. Nasty one too,' – adding with relish: 'Real beauty! I'm afraid you'll have to have the three back teeth out.'

'But surely,' I pleaded, 'even if you can't lance the gum, you only need to pull one tooth, the one near the trouble?'

' 'Fraid not.' He shook his head. 'All three are pretty bad. Better have 'em all out. Can't answer for the consequences if you don't.'

There was nothing to be done. I looked despairingly at his instruments lying among the flies on a piece of cloth, and weakly insisted on an injection of penicillin as well as novocaine, a request that seemed to hurt his feelings. He injected, then left me to deal with another patient while I lay back waiting for the novocaine to take effect.

It took him nearly forty-five minutes to extract the first tooth – in five pieces. At the end, worried by the odd trifles that remained behind, he gouged around with a scalpel.

'Pretty rotten teeth.' He wiped the sweat on his forehead with his sleeve. 'Pretty bad shape, I'm afraid.'

As a rule the dentist's chair holds no fears for me, but I was terrified at the prospect of going through this burrowing and cutting twice more. The poor dentist was also exhausted. He was drenched. He looked inside my mouth again and then he straightened up. He had come to a decision.

'Well,' he announced roughly, 'perhaps this will stop the pain for a week or two. When will you be able to see your own dentist?'

I said perhaps in a fortnight.

'They've got to come out, no doubt about it. Pretty rotten teeth, I'm afraid. But I think I've cured the worst of the pain. Try and bear it till you get home.'

I jumped out of his chair with alacrity, perfectly prepared to stand any pain. I paid him $10 for his exertions and ran out – waiting for the toothache. It never came. And I still have the other two teeth. But it was a narrow squeak. He would have had the lot out if he hadn't suddenly lost heart.

The interlude with my friendly neighbourhood dentist was kid stuff, but the car crash (for which I was exonerated from blame in the French courts) taught me one fact of life that may console those who fear death, particularly violent death. Don't worry. Romeo had it in the right perspective when he said, 'How oft when men are at the point of death have they been merry!'

I will not go so far as to say that death is a cheerful business, but I do know one thing. I have all but died several times, and I have never had time to be frightened; not because I am courageous, but because, as I really have discovered the hard way, the human brain has a built-in mechanism that blocks out fear in moments of crisis.

After all, when the French car hit mine on that lonely French road, five of us blacked out at precisely the same split second of impact. In a sense I 'died' just as dreadful a death as the unfortunate four who were killed. By a miracle, I woke up. But is there any reason to suppose that the four people in the other car, in their last sad moments on earth, should have been stricken by any more fear than I was? For my last remembered thoughts before I 'died' were, 'There goes the bloody holiday!' I had no time to think I might die.

Similar inconsequential thoughts crowded my mind when I was flying back by night from India in a Boeing 707 at 35,000 feet, and without warning was jolted out of a drugged sleep by an almost unbearable pressure on my chest, as though strong arms were pinioning me. I thought at first it was a heart attack – and that *did* frighten me. But then, as I struggled to a sitting position, a cascade of pots and pans, knives and forks, cups and saucers hurtled past me like a scene from an outrageous custard-pie comedy, and crashed against the bulkhead behind the pilot's cabin. A carrier-cot, with a baby in it, flew past. A parcel that had no right to be on the rack – I remember it was square with sharp corners – whizzed past me, hit a man a couple of seats ahead and blood spurted all over the place. As I fought the invisible object sitting on my chest, my brief-case (containing irreplaceable records of weeks of research) seemed to rise in front of me, as though by levitation; I tried to grab it, but it was swept away into the stream of objects whistling among the screaming passengers.

At last I realised that we were going straight down, nose first, straight down, out of control. I groped in my pocket, with only one thought in my mind. I had spent my last few thousand rupees on a gorgeous gem-studded bracelet for Titina. Now I realised I was going to die, and before the pressure blacked me out, I gripped the bracelet in my right-hand jacket pocket, and swore, 'If some bastard tries to steal this from my body, he'll have to cut off my arm.'

Seconds later – minutes? hours? immeasurable time – the pain in my chest suddenly eased. I felt 'free'. Dimly I heard the Aussie pilot announce, a trifle breathlessly, 'No cause for alarm, ladies and gentlemen. Sorry about all the trouble, but everything's under control now.' It took me two minutes to unclench my hand from the bracelet in my pocket. I just could not unlock my fingers.

Apparently (though I never heard this officially) the gyroscope had slipped its moorings and we dived fifteen thousand feet – luckily over the Baluchistan desert, which contains no inconvenient mountains. The pilot did not dare bring the plane out of the dive too quickly in case he wrenched off a wing.

We limped into Bahrain at 4 a.m. Sixty people had to receive medical treatment, and in the sandy garden out-side the hot airport building, an extraordinary collection of objects that had been wrenched from people by the pressures of the dive awaited collection. I found my brief-case. Still bemused, I suddenly saw a shoe that looked uncommonly like one made by Mr Lobb. I had not until that moment realised that a shoe had been mysteriously plucked from my foot.

I was luckier than some of the others, in particular those who perhaps gave an involuntary cry when the dive started, for among the objects waiting to be collected on the table in the garden were four sets of false teeth.

But I never had time to be afraid.

17

ADVICE FROM A
VIRGIN SOLDIER

IT TOOK ME many years of failure disguised as modest
success to discover that, though I could string words together
as a foreign correspondent, I needed to do much
more than that if I ever hoped to write an even moderately
good book. I had tried; the failure was disguised because
after a certain time as a correspondent (and with several
TV documentaries to my credit) I *could* sell every book I
suggested writing. I would think of an idea based on some
of my travels, and it would be immediately accepted by a
publisher, doubtless because of my byline in the *Daily
Mail*. But nobody seemed to buy many copies.

In my innocence, or vanity, I blithely assumed that if
ten per cent of the *Daily Mail*'s five million or so readers
who identified me with a given adventurous assignment
wanted to read a fuller version in book form, I would have
a best-seller on my hands. It was an attitude of mind that
often led me to take the easy way out.

When I spent several weeks at the Pole in 1957, a
publisher managed to get a radio message to me offering
me an agreeable four-figure advance for my story of the
Fuchs–Hillary trans-Antarctic expedition. They naturally
wanted to publish it before Fuchs's official account and
because of the American involvement, my book would
certainly be published in the United States. I started work
on it in my plastic hut at the Pole, and actually finished it
in the Avenida Palace Hotel in Barcelona, where after
my return (and a short holiday) I went to cover some
anti-Franco riots. There was nothing for it but to get up at
5 a.m. each day and work for several hours before changing

176

hats. Had I really seized the opportunity, I would have done a year's homework before putting pen to paper and tried to write a major book about the exploit, relating it to the Antarctic of Scott, Amundsen, Mawson and others, perhaps working in my feelings and observations as a background to the exploits of Hillary and Fuchs. Instead I rattled off the same dreary old 'I was there' story and pocketed my American and British advances, while the book fell into the nearest crevasse.

I came to earth with a bump after the car crash laid me up for nearly twelve months. Temporarily (I hoped) I became syndication manager of the *Daily Mail* group. At first I wallowed in misery, dreaming of travel, the smell of the sea, the click-clunk of a plane's safety belts, the special excitement that comes when a bellhop carries your suitcase into a strange hotel bedroom in a remote country. Soon it became apparent that I would never return to the life of a foreign correspondent. What I did not realise at first was that this ill wind would have the direct effect of enabling me to achieve my first ambition, of becoming a writer. Not yet fiction, but still . . .

Until this natural break I had written books between assignments. Now, suddenly, that life had gone, and the outlook seemed bleak until I received some invaluable advice: I must stop hating my desk. I must use it! Don't be in such a rush. I must take a couple of years to write my next book.

I hesitated at first. I had started out in life being paid to do one job while I worked on my books in my spare time. Now life had come full circle; I was back where I started, working in an office and *still* writing in my spare time.

It seemed as though I would never win, yet in the end I decided to take the advice; I must take advantage of my desk. I would experiment by writing a book on a subject that intrigued me, set in an area of the world for which I felt sympathy, and then take a year to research it before starting to write. It was a big decision, for I had passed fifty.

One evening the idea came to me: the Black Hole of Calcutta. I knew the city well; indeed I am one of the few people who enjoy visiting it. I had read Holroyd's description of the terrible night in 1756, and wondered why no one had written a more detailed account of the events leading up to the actual night in the Black Hole. I started browsing among the records and was fascinated by the amount of material available. What is more, it was all in London, an important consideration when my presence was requested at the office five days a week.

There was no point in going half-measures, in trying to produce a book as a spare-time hobby. Once I decided on the subject I set the alarm for 6 a.m., and the next morning started a new seven-days-a-week pattern. I reached the office at 7 a.m., toiled at research until 10 when it opened; some days I snatched another two hours by having a sandwich lunch, and on Saturdays and Sundays I hardly smelt fresh air. I loved every moment of it.

I had no illusions that I could or would produce a story that would live for more than a few months. All I hoped to do was to improve on the past (a hope not always fulfilled). I was not seeking the fame that Austin Dobson found to be 'a food that dead men eat'.

Leslie Thomas had some interesting advice. 'Get everything – *anything* – on paper before you forget it,' he urged me, 'or even worse, before you dry up.' Like many of us Leslie, an ex-Barnardo boy, has a genuine fear that the day may come when he will not be able to write another book – this despite the huge success of his book, *The Virgin Soldiers*, a hilarious story based on his experiences as a conscript in Malaya, which was made into a very successful film. An extrovert who sports a handsome Zapata moustache, Leslie at times became so depressed at the prospect of drying up that he did something practical about it. I discovered this when the two of us had to spend a night in Norwich recording an Anglia TV programme.

We had only to speak for a few minutes each, and on the morning of the shooting Leslie asked if he could be interviewed first. On the way to the studio he turned to me saying, 'See you in the hotel for dinner tonight.' That was at 9.30 a.m. and Leslie vanished for ten hours. The following morning when we caught the train back to London, Leslie arrived at the station followed by a porter struggling under the weight of a bulging kitbag.

'What on earth's in there?' I asked.

'Silver!' replied Leslie cheerfully. 'I hired a car yesterday and went round the villages buying all the silver I could find.'

'But surely if you want a few knives and forks, you could get them in the Portobello Road?'

With a touch of mock hauteur Leslie retorted, 'I do not *buy* silver in the Portobello Road, I *sell* there.'

As a hedge against a shortage of ideas Leslie had bought a stall in London's famous street of bargains and (at the time of writing) works there with his wife every Saturday morning. His prices are quite reasonable, and if you mention my name, you might get ten per cent discount.

What I really needed most of all was down-to-earth criticism. When an author has put everything he knows into a book, it is difficult for him to respond effectively to general criticism. One very discerning friend read a few early chapters of *Calcutta* and wrote, 'Much of the book is fine, but don't you think there is something wrong with chapters 3 and 5? They seem to be diffuse – I wonder if you could pull them together a bit, tighten them. Read them again and you'll see what I mean.' But how can one 'read again' with any critical judgement words that have danced before one's eyes for weeks?

But then came another letter which started, 'Great – with reservations. Here are some points: Why not try to cut twenty per cent out of chapter three? Why not take out the whole of the second incident? And there isn't enough dialogue – none at all in chapter five – to carry the action forward. And when you describe the Hooghly River I can see it, but I don't smell it. What about the street smells? Calcutta must smell! There's room for a paragraph of smells.' There was much more in the same vein.

These two letters are from my files. The first was written by a literary friend, the second by the late James Kinross, a novelist in his own right who became my agent in London until he died.

Dear, wonderful Jamie. In many ways he was the closest friend I had. He had an extraordinary ability to seize on any weaknesses in a manuscript and explain what was needed in a few sentences. Tall, handsome, pipe-smoking, always immaculate in bowler and yellow gloves, he was on a full-disability pension following a war wound and fought a gallant battle against illness until finally after dinner one night he went quietly to bed and died.

Jamie was not only prodigal with advice but was generous with his own actual words. When I was striving in vain to reconstruct a battle scene in *Calcutta*, Jamie sent me a copy of one of his novels with a note, 'Take a look at chapter six. I think it's just what you need. Use as much of it as you like. No one seems to have bought it, so you needn't bother to change the words, apart from changing Africa to India.'

It was rather sad to reflect that when I was young and trying so hard, I had no friends to whom I could turn, and now, by luck I suppose, everybody was trying to help. Jamie's advice was backed up by one of the editors at Collins, who had agreed to publish the book. Milton Waldman was a quietly spoken American whose flair had been responsible for many a Collins best-seller, and he was generous with his help – all of it very practical.

I produced a list of goods Holroyd was buying to take to Calcutta; but a list is a list, and cannot be anything but dull. 'Put Holroyd in the shops where he bought the stuff,' suggested Milton. 'Find out how much things cost in those days, and it will give you a chance to switch scenes from India to London – a break for the reader.'

I rewrote the chapter and it did come alive. Later I faced a different problem when I had to account for several years when nothing really happened. 'Forget it,' said Milton. 'It's got nothing to do with the book.'

Though Jamie and Milton tried their best, the first draft of *Calcutta* was so bad that I could do only one thing. After writing 25,000 words I tore the pages up and started to write the book all over again.

'Splendid!' cried Jamie when we lunched that day. And though the eventual result was not splendid, at least the book – the first of many 'reconstructions' I was to write – was chosen by a book club, sold well, and even, to my surprise, went into paperback in America. It is still bringing in royalties many years after publication.

I write with some feeling about the need for detailed criticism, because before I met Jamie I wrote a book in hospital after the car crash ('Good therapy,' said the doctor) called *Life With Titina*. I still believe that, had I been guided by a good editor, it might well have been successful, for it told a good story. I could feel in my bones (those that were left intact) that it should have had the same appeal as *The Egg and I*. The material was there. What I needed was an enthusiastic, but not too sympathetic, friend to sit on the end of the bed – well, near the bed – and tell me to tear up some chapters, rewrite others, expand some, cut some. Instead, not a word was rewritten. I never had a single word of discussion with anyone about it. It was published. Titina bought most of the copies for friends, and the book sank without trace.

Yet critics – especially one's friends – can be so wrong. In my early days I had no friends in the book trade, but during the war I met Elizabeth Bowen, that master of the short story, after she had reviewed a book I had written about my journey across Siberia by train; as the book was published at the time Russia entered the war, it had a certain topicality. Elizabeth and I became firm friends. She was tall, angular, rather plain, but with a warm smile that lit up her face, and our friendship continued long after I had moved to Paris.

It was in Paris that I spent my spare moments writing

some account of my early life, and I sent a copy of the
finished work to Elizabeth for her opinion. I shall never
forget the morning her reply arrived and the excitement
with which I read her first words: 'It's wonderful!' It was,
she was convinced, one of the best books of its kind she
had ever read. She had obviously perused it page by page,
for she singled out certain passages and discussed them.
Hastily I wrapped up the top copy and sent it to Spencer
Curtis Brown, at that time my agent.

His reply was devastating. The book was no good. It
was long-winded, it had no character, it was like going to
a cocktail party and meeting everybody without getting
to know anyone. I was shattered, for I had banked on
Elizabeth's judgement, and when next I was in London I
showed Spencer the letter she had written to me.

'Oh, Elizabeth,' said Spencer rather sadly. 'She's the
most wonderful woman in the world, but never ask her for
an opinion. She's so kind-hearted she can't bear to say
anything horrible to a friend.'

There was nothing to be done. I threw the manuscript
away.

Even the judgement of tough critics in publishing
houses, whose very existence depends on encouraging
writers, finding new talent and helping it along, is fallible.
A successful publisher is as much a gambler as a successful
poker player, particularly when he is asked to commission
a project of which nothing more than a synopsis has been
written. When *Calcutta* was in proof, I had the notion of
writing a book on the fall of Singapore in 1941. I hoped to
produce an accurate, blow-by-blow account of an historic
defeat in a part of the world I knew and loved well. I was
not deterred by the fact that scores of books had already
been written on the great Japanese victory. I drafted a
synopsis and sent it to my publishers.

Billy Collins was enthusiastic about the idea, but Milton
Waldman who had helped me with *Calcutta* was not. There
was nothing new to be written about it, he said. All I could
hope to do was to milk other people's books and string

together a few official reports. Fortunately Billy overruled him, and *Sinister Twilight* became one of the most success-ful books I have written.

18

THE LOST LANDS OF ESCAPE

IT WAS RAINING on that wintry day in 1964 when I returned to my office in Fleet Street after lunch at the Wig and Pen. The unopened letter, marked Personal, was lying on the desk. I took a glance at the garish stamp and a forgotten world came rushing back to me: Rarotonga, the dawdling capital of the Cook Islands in the South Pacific.

I was in my fifties, shackled to a desk. True, the work was not arduous, and gave me plenty of time to write books which were achieving a modest success. True, I was happy being able at long last to write, but there is a difference between happiness and contentment. The transition from life lived out of a suitcase to the life of an armchair traveller is not easy; in a way my writing was like a talcum powder to help soothe itchy feet that never quite stopped itching.

I was not complaining. I had a beautiful wife, two children, a warm and happy home, a cottage and five acres in the country, and a life behind me that most men would envy. I had no wistful longings to return to the rigours of a foreign correspondent's job; but occasionally, particularly when it rained, I longed to be in Singapore or San Francisco.

My brooding thoughts had been intensified a few weeks before this when an old friend in the office had been seized with a bout of coughing while smoking; as we carried him into the ambulance, suffering from a stroke, I decided to give up the sixty Gauloises a day that were making *me* cough. It was my cough that frightened me, and sure enough after a week of no-smoking misery it stopped. It really did. For all of two days. And then, dammit, I caught whooping cough. So I was in a gloomy mood when I opened the letter. It was from Tom Neale, the rawboned misfit of a New Zealander I had visited on the tiny coral island of Suvarov in the centre of the Pacific Ocean. As I read his letter, the instamatic camera of the brain produced an image of the moment I had first seen the island, in the bluest of blue lagoons, edged by white sand framed in tall, slender, bending palms. I remembered the fun Tom and I had together, spearing fish and cooking breadfruit, drinking coconut milk after a swim.

In the letter Tom told me how he had been taken ill on the island, and was preparing for a lonely death when a small American yacht anchored by chance in the lagoon, and gave him passage to Raro, where he faced months of convalescence before he could return to the island – if ever. 'What about my book?' he wrote. 'You remember you said you would help me. Have you got three months to spare?'

The answer was obviously no. Fifty-five is no age to start trifling with one's job. Yet Tom offered me this half-chance to realise a hitherto unfulfilled dream: to live and work, however briefly, in the South Seas, to experience something more than the tantalising glimpses I had had before. I wanted to be a part of life in the South Seas as I had been in Singapore, the Middle and Far East, and above all, I wanted to taste the delights of that most wondrous of islands, Tahiti, or even better, its tiny neighbour Moorea.

But three months! Time is far more precious than money. I brooded over tentative plans. I knew that my deputy in the syndication department, Vyvyan Bell, was more capable than I was of running the office. I knew that I had a good 'track record' with the company; we had served each other well. Dare I ask for a sabbatical? I had never presumed upon my friendship with Esmond Rothermere – and I had no intention of doing so now.

I had to find a different way. I talked the problem over with Titina. She had spent month after month alone when I was a foreign correspondent but now that we lived in

London she had many more friends; and, too, I was not going to dash off into the unknown for months on end. She knew I had itchy feet – but at least they were itchy only to travel in order to write. Besides, with her Italian attitude to marriage she felt that the basic, utterly selfish recipe for a long and happy married life is for the wife to make sure the husband is happy.

'You've earned good money from *Calcutta*,' she said. 'Why don't you ask the *Mail* if you could work only nine months a year?'

I did just that. Once my publisher had agreed to finance a visit to Tahiti – which I was able to convince him was the only possible place to meet Tom Neale – I saw 'Duke' Hussey, managing director of the *Mail*, gulped once or twice and asked if I could have my salary reduced by 25 per cent in return for a new contract under which I would work only nine months a year.

He didn't hesitate. 'Why not?' he said. 'I'll get a new contract drawn up right away.' And as I reached the door he asked, 'Want anyone to carry your bags?' And so, thanks to 'Duke', I was able to start a new life at fifty-five.

Two weeks later I flew to Tahiti. Tom, skinnier than ever, mahogany-brown and looking slightly unreal with his trousers on, was waiting at the airport, and as soon as I had cleared my bags we drove into Papeete for breakfast.

It seems fashionable nowadays for travellers to denigrate Papeete as a sleazy slum; dirty and tatty though it may be, it still has the attraction of a one-time beauty run to seed but whose early bloom is clearly discernible beneath the make-up. Anyway, one expects to see a certain tawdriness in the islands of the South Seas; it is part of the charm of the happy-go-lucky inhabitants that rags become them as much as riches.

Tom and I stopped for breakfast at the Café Denise on the main waterfront street, a few tables on the pavement sandwiched between Chinese shops and the more important French buildings, the Banque Nationale, a ship's chandlers, the PTT. A long line of ancient trees, as imposing as any plane trees in a French provincial town, broke the view of the still lagoon, shining in the early morning like a pewter dish.

The *patron* brought us ham and eggs, served in the French manner, in the small metal skillet in which they had been cooked. Even the coffee tasted French, it was so bad. As in Saigon, the French influence blended perfectly with the local characteristics, but it was never as dominant as it used to be in British colonies. It had just happened. Along the main street facing the lagoon the road bustled with French cars and Vespas, and at each corner a policeman in khaki blew his shrill whistle and waved as fiercely as any Paris *flic*, encouraging everyone to drive more quickly.

Near the Custom House, from which our launch would depart, one enormous mango and several scarlet flame trees shaded a trough where women were washing clothes, as in any French mountain village, though here they did not lay them on stones to dry, but hung them haphazardly on a near-by clump of bamboo. As the morning boat from Moorea entered the passage through the reef, then approached the pier, a crowd of chattering men and women, dressed in dazzling colours, waited to greet it. They were not passengers, not friends or relatives, just people. I was entranced.

Tom saw the scene through different eyes. 'Come on,' he said as the boat tied up. 'This place stinks.'

A few minutes later I was aboard the morning launch for the three-hour trip to Moorea, where years before Tom had lived and worked. By lunchtime I was in my own 'home', a three-room attap-roofed hut, near a clump of bending palms and only five yards away from the creamy foam of the gently breaking waves.

Oblong like most Moorean houses, the hut had walls of bamboo, so tightly packed they kept out the rain, yet let in the air and light. There were no windows, only doors with rattan curtains, and by the front door stood a large ochre pot of water with a cheap, gaudily painted metal dish by its side – the Tahitian equivalent of the boot-scraper in front of an English country home. After walking on the beach I simply poured water over my feet before entering the house.

Though ostensibly a 'native' hut, it had been skilfully modernised. The bathroom had a shower; there was electric light. The kitchen had a cooker and a gas refrigerator. Two laughing girls had been engaged to cook and keep house, and René, the brother of one of the girls, explained in French that each morning he would inquire what kind of fish I wanted for lunch, whereupon he would go and catch it. One of the two small, delightful, non-chromium hotels on the island was a quarter of a mile walk along the beach. I knew it was not for ever. Yet I felt as Gauguin must have felt when he landed on Tahiti in the days when it was like Moorea, with no airfield and thus not ruined by mass tourism.

'Like it?' asked Tom, and when I nodded, he added, 'Shall we start work after lunch?'

I looked at the backdrop of blue and green volcanic mountains tumbling down to the narrow fringes of beach girdling Captain Cook Bay, the tiny garden behind the hut blazing with hibiscus, oleander, and heady with the sensuous perfume of the small white, star-shaped tiare, the flower of the island, growing on its bush of thick green leaves.

The girls were preparing lunch of *mahi mahi*, fried fillets of flying fish, and yams with, instead of bread, scones made of *uto* – the soft kernel that grows inside the young coconut before turning to milk – cooked with breadfruit from a tree in the garden. Someone had picked some fresh grapefruit, each one the size of a football, and a wooden bowl was filled with wild red bananas.

'No, Tom.' I sipped some coconut milk laced with gin. 'Sorry, but life begins at fifty-five – and for one week in my life I'm going to be a beachcomber.'

It was paradise. Some mornings I went with René to collect clams for lunch, or spear fish in the motionless lagoon where one could stand and watch fish of every imaginable colour and stripe, darting like butterflies in the clear water. René could remain motionless for half an hour, waiting until a big fish approached, then, all in one moment, he leaned forward, the spear moved, there was a flurry in the water, and out came a silvery lunch. At other times he and his friends took a canoe and paddled outside the many-coloured coral reef into the white foamy waves that battered against it. If lucky, they caught a really big fish, sometimes a tunny, sometimes a dolphin, which (like swordfish) makes one of the most succulent steaks in the world. They buried the fish in the sand until it was time to cut it up and share the steaks just before lunch.

There were no telephones, only radio contact once a day with Papeete. In the evening I watched the flying fish leaping by the dozen, and after dark played chess in the hotel until the electricity was switched off at 10 p.m. There was one cinema show a week, on Sunday evening, but I never went. A handful of French and Americans lived in Moorea, but because the island was cut off from tourists, the whites were absorbed by the islanders, instead of imposing their way of life on the inhabitants with their small houses, a sewing machine in front of nearly every door, and at the end of each village the white patch of a church.

No white man wanted to change such an idyllic way of life. The French manager of the hotel, my chess opponent, and his American assistant had settled down to wedded bliss with island girls, without going through the ceremony of marriage – though they may be formally married by now, because the Tahitians have their rules. These two couples were, to use the local French word, *marié* — but only inasmuch as they lived together. They had children. If they were still in love when the children grew up, then they might go to a priest and become *marié-marié*. It was a trial marriage – for ten or fifteen years; not always a perfect compromise in our civilisation, but comparatively painless in the islands of the South Seas, where money is not absolutely essential, so that if a girl goes back to mother there is enough food for all. To the Tahitians love is not acquisitive, not demanding. When a girl gets *marié* she is entering into a happy association which she could not consider continuing if she were no longer happy.

It seems a very moral way of living to me, and often it is the girls who are afraid to marry white men legally at first. Too many whites have fallen for the alluring girls of the South Seas, married them in the small white church, then yearned for 'civilisation', forcing an island wife to choose between living in a hateful city or being left on the island still married and so ruining her chances of remarrying.

I left Moorea only once in three months, to attend a party given by an American bachelor called Jack Donaldson, who lived just outside Papeete. I took the launch over for the night, for to my mind Donaldson, whom I had first met when working in San Francisco, had (with the advantage of money), solved the tedious problems of living to perfection. He spent six months a year in San Francisco, three months in Europe, and three months in his house outside Papeete.

A taxi stopped at the gates of a garden filled with banks of bougainvillaea, frangipani and tiare. Inside the house I goggled at a bevy of girls apparently unattached, unaffected, and beautiful. Long black hair, decorated with hibiscus, fell over their shoulders. One strummed a guitar, one sang, one very beautiful girl in a red and white pareu took my arm gently, led me to a table and offered me one of the world's greatest cocktail dips, raw fish marinated in limes and onions.

Though the degree of beauty varied, all had what I can only call 'style'. They moved gracefully. Their manners were impeccable. Innocently I presumed they were the daughters of our host's friends, but in fact they had arrived just before I did in an old bus, for when Donaldson gave a party he invariably invited a busload of *vahines*, the easy-going ladies of Tahiti.

The *vahines* were *not* 'professionals' in our sense of the word. As James Ramsey Ullman, the American author, wrote, 'By their own lights they are thoroughly decent and self-respecting *vahines*. It is their light, not ours, that makes the rule of the road in Tahiti.'

People ask me if it's true that the *vahines* bestow their favours gladly and warmly on lonely white men. The answer is an absolute and enthusiastic affirmative – with one condition. The girl has to like you – that is the crux of the Tahitian code of morals, and it is this that prevents the girls from becoming brassy tarts. But if one of them does like a man – and there is usually *one* who does – then he will want for nothing more of life than to stay in the South Seas for ever. For any relationship is based on one elemental fact – that she is a woman, and her task in life is to please a man. To the Tahitian, making love is as natural as breathing or sleeping.

Back in London, I could now look forward to travelling three months a year, and during the next five or six years I wrote three books, each one of which needed research in exciting countries. *Sinister Twilight* told the story of the fall of Singapore in 1942; *From the Land of Lost Content* described the flight of the Dalai Lama from Tibet; this was followed by *The War of the Running Dogs*, the twelve-year 'Emergency' in Malaya when the Communists tried to take over the country.

Apart from the hard slog of the actual writing, these books satisfied two deep desires: travel to destinations chosen by myself; and a continuation at a slower tempo of the life of a foreign correspondent. For I was still searching out stories and characters, battling with officials in dreary foreign government offices. But having unearthed my characters, I was not haunted by the correspondent's recurring nightmare of getting the story back to head office before a rival, making sure of one's lines of communication, of stresses that create their own imperatives. Now all I had to do was search for news (of a sort) at half-speed, with a day off whenever I felt like it – a task much more suited to an elderly gentleman, but still, in essence, similar to the work I had been doing all over the world for so many years.

It was wonderful to return to Singapore, which has gripped my imagination since the day in 1938 when I first set foot on the island. Outwardly much had changed, but my eyes did not really see the new skyscrapers and wide roads. I arrived with a tattered old photograph that I had carried (if only in my mind) for thirty years and *that* looked the same. At the end of a haircut a pretty Chinese with a piece of wire asked me, 'Now you wantee ears cleaned?' *That* was Singapore. When I stayed with an old friend, T. W. Ong, an Oxford educated barrister (the best there is in Singapore), in his large house in a compound, a census officer found seventy relations of Ong's six servants living behind the house and eating off the Ong grocery bill. *That* was Singapore.

When I walked the streets, each one still led to the sight of ships shimmering on the horizon, a passenger liner surrounded by sampans, or an ancient, overworked, rusted freighter being loaded by an endless human conveyor belt. The Singapore River still twisted through the heart of the city, alive with sampans on which men, women and children lived and died. It still dispensed its potent smell compounded of drains, swampland, dried fish, plus a score of spices that lay waiting to be unloaded from the junks with their patched brown sails – junks that had sailed north from the spice islands. The smell is not unpleasant, but once smelt it is never forgotten.

Each morning I awoke to the hot, wet, smell of a new day in the tropics, while in TW's compound nothing had changed. There were still intriguing glimpses of attap huts, palm trees, broad green banana leaves, or wild sago, its fronds like feathers, and papaya, the trees so frail it was hard to believe they could bear such heavy fruit. As dusk fell, and I sat with a stengah on a cane chair, with extensions for my legs, the cicadas and bullfrogs started their noises, somehow giving me the impression of up-country jungle far removed from any city. The essential charm of Singapore – that the jungle of the city never quite swallows the jungle that surrounds it – was the same. Even on the Bukit Timah Road, one of the main streets, I picked orchids by the roadside. And one evening at the Tanglin Club, drinking my stengah on the veranda, I saw three monkeys lope off into the woods and climb into the lacy foliage of a casuarina tree.

Perhaps it was my deep love for Singapore that helped to make *Sinister Twilight* more successful than any other book I had written until then; thirteen years after it was originally published it has been reprinted eight or nine times and is still selling briskly in paperback. No one knows what makes a best-seller, because the next book, about the flight of the Dalai Lama seemed to have similar ingredients – tragedy, a sympathetic readership, plus a certain mysticism, yet it did not sell as well.

At first I wondered if people instinctively refused to buy it out of a subconscious guilt complex, a sense that the West had done nothing to save a country from rape; but the fault went deeper. I realise now that I failed to surmount an elementary writing problem. I had been unable to get under the skins of the characters because I never really understood them. The material was as exciting as in *Twilight*, but in that book official ineptness had been merely a backdrop to the reactions of living characters. The ordinary men and women of Singapore, whose story I had been writing, came alive because I was able to communicate with them, share their feelings, so that unconsciously perhaps I put myself in their place when writing the book. In my book on Tibet the characters had no life, and no writer can make even the most exciting events come alive if every man and woman is, as Sheridan put it, 'a character dead at every word'.

Fortunately there was a compensation, the remarkable experience of spending some time with the Dalai Lama, who was living quietly in exile at Dharmsala, a hill town in north-west India, and I had a stroke of luck when the *Reader's Digest* decided, on the strength of my story outline, to buy the serial rights before the book was written: this meant that they would help to pay for the research, which in turn meant that my old friend Donald Dinsley, who had helped me for many years with various research projects, could accompany me to India. Spending some weeks with a God-King is no laughing matter, yet the time that Din and I spent in India had some hilarious moments, starting with my arrival.

Din had flown from London before me to make certain there would be no government interference, for the Dalai Lama was a refugee in India and the Indians have always been terrified of the Chinese; I knew that Indian officials might question my journey, even delay me, unless I was armed with the right piece of paper.

There were no problems. Din arranged with the government in Delhi to cable the High Commission in London, which issued me with a letter of authority, explaining to even the dumbest civil servant that the purpose of my visit was to interview and *photograph* the Dalai Lama. I had stressed to a mystified Din that he make it clear that I wanted to take photographs. I had *not* mentioned the fact that I possess only one camera, the simplest and cheapest that money can buy.

I landed at Delhi at 4 a.m. When I showed my letter I was gracefully waved through the customs, and no one opened a suitcase or queried the contents of my extremely heavy hand luggage. There was no reason why they should, for it was clearly marked, 'Fragile – developing fluid'; that was why I had to carry it. Once in the concourse Din grabbed the case, took one look at the label and asked, 'What's all this photography lark?'

'Careful,' I whispered; 'there are six bottles of Scotch in there.' Whisky costs £9 a bottle in India.

All went well until I saw a customs officer chasing me. 'I am going to be asking you about your developing fluid,' he lilted. Dinsley looked at me. I prepared to confess all;

but the Indian continued, 'You are a professional, I know this from the document, but I must be telling you that I am a very high-grade amateur, and would request your help.'

As I prepared to invent my qualifications he added, 'No, no, sir, not that at all; but in this country our developing fluid is of such poor quality I beseech you, sir, to spare me a bottle of your precious fluid?'

Din was magnificent. Without hesitation he prepared to undo the case, and then, just at the right moment, looked up as though he had forgotten, and said, 'But, Noel – you told me the bottles had to be hermetically sealed until we get to Dharmsala.' We promised to send the customs officer a supply when we opened the first bottle, then bolted for the exit.

Din had arranged the first series of interviews for a few days hence, including one at Mussoorie, north of Dehra Dun in the Himalayan foothills, and on the way to Dharmsala. There was no point in asking for a railway guide. I walked up to the rank of decrepit taxis, picked out what appeared to be the cleanest and said, 'Taxi.'

'Yes, sahib,' cried the driver. 'I am waiting to be of service to you.'

'I've got a long trip ahead of me,' I warned him, 'and I have to start right now.'

'No matter, sahib,' he lilted, 'wherever you wish to go in our magnificent continent I will be taking you.'

And he did. In the first five days we travelled fourteen hundred miles by cab.

Dharmsala was – and no doubt still is – a small, flinty township high up in the mountains north-west of Amritsar, and consists chiefly of a ragged main street lined with poor shops, fruit stalls and one cinema. The Dalai Lama had promised all the help he could give us, but there was no room for us to stay in his court in the village of Upper Dharmsala, a few thousand feet higher up the mountain. It was better in a way to be on our own, particularly as Dharmsala boasted an ornamental maharajah's palace which had been converted into a government resthouse.

We reached the town shortly before sundown, and drove through a handsome if untended garden to the resplendent front portico. My first forebodings came when we entered the hall which was thick with dirt. They increased when we were told rooms cost the equivalent of only 50p a night. For this modest sum we were offered, 'Two rooms, sahib, each with private bath.'

Din had a bedroom straight out of the Arabian Nights, with a bathroom tiled in blue mosaic and with gold-plated taps. The fact that the taps never worked did not worry anyone. I had a bathroom with ordinary kitchen taps which *did* work, but there were no plugs in either the basin or bath. And there was not one single plug to be bought in Dharmsala. We took the gold-plated plugs out of Din's bathroom and used them in mine. On the other hand Din had a bedside lamp, producing a sombre, dim glow from a 30-watt bulb, whereas my light dangled on a short flex from a domed ceiling so high that, in order to read my notes after dusk, I had to stand on the bed.

Our bearer was kind, polite and willing. He also had such terrible BO that when he brought my morning tea, I could smell him as he approached on my balcony. On an empty stomach this was more than I could take, so I introduced him to what I explained was an English custom reserved for the servants of the aristocracy. At the end of my veranda I left each evening a large bottle of Roger & Gallet – *Extra Vieille*, nothing but the best – which I had picked up at a duty-free shop. He daubed his person liberally with this each morning to our mutual satisfaction.

We only ate breakfast in our sumptuous surroundings, but even that simple meal had its hazards. The attractive dining room overlooking the valley had huge windows framed in rich crimson curtains, weighted with dust. The plates and cutlery were beautiful – each piece with its own special pattern of thumb marks. We bought a supply of paper napkins to clean knives and forks and cups, but what to do about bacon and egg served on filthy plates?

I overcame this by introducing another 'English' custom – fried bacon on toast, with boiled eggs as a side dish. Only in the 'best' houses, I insisted, did milords and ladies breakfast in such unusual fashion. Try it if you ever find yourself in Dharmsala. The boiled egg *had* to be clean, and I could clean the egg spoon. The bacon never touched the dirty plate, and of course I never ate the toast, explaining that, in the same way rich Chinese always leave the rice for the domestics, rich English lords always, by tradition, leave the toast for the bearers. Before long all the guests were being served bacon on toast and the bearers never had it so good.

One morning, though, the grime on my coffee cup was so thick that I blew up and shouted, 'Look at this bloody cup! It's a disgrace.'

The bearer looked really chagrined – as though the honour of India had been insulted. 'I am utterly sorry, *burra sahib*,' he cried. 'I apologise most humbly for this episode, and I shall rectify it immediately.'

He did. He grabbed the cup, made his way to the magnificent dining room windows, wiped the cup thoroughly on the crimson curtains, handing it back to me with a smile of quiet triumph.

I approached the Dalai Lama with awe. All that I knew about him, and the strange circumstances in which he had been chosen, had been culled from books, supplemented by the personal experiences of an old friend, Heinrich Harrer who wrote *Seven Years in Tibet*. When lunching with me in London, Heinie had promised only that I would be surprised – and delighted. I wondered what to expect.

I *was* delighted. To me it was like meeting a saint – only a saint with a sense of humour, a saint with the common touch. Still in his thirties when we met, the Dalai Lama had a serious face which broke into sudden warm, serene smiles.

At our first meeting he looked younger than later, for he had closely cropped hair which the following week he shaved for some religious ceremony. He wore glasses, because of the years he had spent studying in the ill-lit rooms of the Potala in Lhasa, study which resulted in an extraordinary grasp of international affairs, of places, names, books, dates. All had been learned from books; and if – only if – this son of an illiterate peasant had become Dalai Lama as a result of some devious chicanery, or sheer luck, then he proved a staggering illustration of the power of concentrated learning. He told me that he had no difficulty in learning a 300-page book by heart.

Yet his youth, surrounded as he had been by teachers and lamas, must have been lonely and miserable, and that perhaps is why he was so delighted when Harrer arrived and introduced him to mechanical objects like cameras and watches. They were the only toys he was allowed. He was no slouch with a watch, as I discovered during my second week, when casually I mentioned that mine was behaving oddly. He asked to look at it, took off the back and peered into the mysterious world of wheels and springs.

'I see what's the matter.' He spoke quite good English. 'Perhaps I can mend it.'

Before I could say 'Rolex' he had sent for screwdrivers and pliers and there, in the garden courtyard, he took every single piece of the watch out of its case and spread them on a piece of thin muslin. Seeing my dismay, he laughed like a schoolboy, and promised to repair it by the following morning. It has worked perfectly ever since.

I always had a feeling that the Dalai Lama had a hidden humorous streak that he was afraid to show to his awed servitors. He enjoyed manipulating a joke, in the way that he deliberately took my watch to pieces without any warning, to see my reaction. He played rather a different trick for effect some days later. We were in the middle of a long interview when he announced that he had to break off to conduct some special prayers among the lamas who were always milling around his simple house and gardens. I hated the idea of interrupting his train of thought – and mine – so I said, 'May I wait, sir, until you have finished?'

He *knew* I was going to say that. With a mischievous smile – most un-saintlike – he said, 'Of course you may stay, Noel – but these prayers will last eight hours.'

A wonderful man, a man who harboured no bitterness against the Chinese who had uprooted him and destroyed his country. If I had to choose one single word to sum up the Dalai Lama, it would be 'serenity'.

19

TO BE CONTINUED . . .

MY TRIP TO meet the Dalai Lama was the last long foreign journey I made without Titina. Now she travels with me. When we were first married and I set off alone for the Far East, leaving her behind in Switzerland, she warned me politely, 'If you ever go to bed with any of my friends, I'll kill you. But,' she added generously, 'anything you do east of Suez doesn't count.'

A few years ago she said, 'I cancel our previous arrangement. The children are grown up, so now I will travel with you.' The trouble is – old-fashioned though it may seem – we miss each other when apart.

Many old friends and relatives who have appeared in these pages have, alas, disappeared. Titina's Mamie, Mama and Jack, Helen – all have gone. Jack was left a widower at sixty-two and later married again. With his customary panache, he produced, before he died at the age of seventy-four, a half-sister for the brothers Barber. She is just forty years younger than I am.

After taking a diploma in catering, Jane followed in the tradition of the Barbers and joined the RAF as an expert in her field. By early 1977 she had become the only flight lieutenant of whom the erstwhile A/C2 Noel Barber has never been afraid.

Having a young sister can have pitfalls. When I walked this attractive redhead down the King's Road, obviously 'very good friends', I heard one yobbo mutter to his pal, 'Dirty old man, with a kid like that.' Too old to fight for her honour, I riposted haughtily, 'How dare you talk like that in front of my sister.'

Ken has retired from the bank, Tony from politics. But

200

both are still working, Ken as a consultant, Tony as a banker, though where Ken had to start at the bottom, Tony started at the top – as chairman.

Touch wood, Titina and I are happy and healthy; we have two fine children, and I have only had one shaky moment – in 1974, when I was playing tennis for the IC (yes they made me a member) at Biarritz. Suddenly at the start of a match, I found myself retching, my knees buckled, and I thought I was going to pass out.

All's well, I am back on the courts (doubles only), but it was a narrow squeak, and I could have been in trouble had not Teddy Phillips, with whom we were staying, rushed me to his doctor who in turn rushed me to a specialist. He diagnosed fibrillation, an early warning of potential heart trouble, but curable if one takes care.

Titina came with me to the specialist who assured me that there would be no problems providing I returned immediately to England for prolonged treatment. But, he warned me, I must cut out excessive exercise, and above all not get emotionally involved in anything. No violent arguments, no outbursts of temper. *'Pas d'émotion,'* he insisted.

As I was about to go, Titina, who knew that I would never obey orders unless she had heard them and could then enforce them, whispered, 'You'd better ask him about love-making.'

Slightly embarrassed, I shooed her into the waiting room, and asked the doctor, 'What about sex?'

I know the French take their sex very much as a matter of course, rather like food – you need it, and at times a good meal can be memorable. But I was intrigued by his answer.

'Ah, sex,' he mused. 'Tell me, you 'ave ze mistress?'

Rather apologetically I said I didn't.

'Good.' He looked pleased. 'They can be verree emotional. That lady was your wife?' I nodded. ' 'Ow long you are marry?'

I told him twenty years or so.

'Ah well.' He shrugged his shoulders. 'No problem. Carry on as usual. After twenty years it is still verree pleasant, but *pas d'émotion.*'

Of course, he didn't know Titina.

20

. . . BUT NOT CONCLUDED (TOUCH
WOOD)

ONCE WHEN I returned from two months in Central Africa
and Titina and I dined with Esmond, I felt flushed, hot,
and if not actually dizzy, unable to focus with my usual
pleasure on the Guardis that decorated his elegant dining-
room.

That night I had to change the sheets four times. It was
another dose of malaria and it kept me in bed for four
days of sweating agony. And when Titina phoned Esmond
to cancel an appointment, her voice betraying a natural
worry at my condition, Esmond soothed her, 'Don't *worry*,
my dear. Noel is like a cat – he's got nine lives and so far
he's hardly started using them up.'

It seemed that I did have several lives – using up the
first with lockjaw at fifteen, which is usually fatal; but more
important, in a way, was the rare distinction of living
half-a-dozen totally *different* lives, as though I were a
different person, enjoying each one to the full. I had
worked in commerce, I had been supercargo on a tramp
steamer, I had been a reporter, I had even worked on a
secret mission when I was an RAF navigator, then I had
become an editor-in-chief of a prestigious newspaper – a
completely different life. While I edited the *Continental
Daily Mail* I taught myself how to become a magazine
writer in America – writing for magazines like the *Saturday
Evening Post, Holiday, The Reader's Digest*, so that in a
way I compensated for my earlier failed attempts to write
books.

None of this interfered with my work, but it had two
objectives: it increased my earnings, and this second source

of income gave me independence. For much of my life I have earned money from more than one source because I have always been afraid that I might one day be fired. Editors of national newspapers are quirky people, often the first to be fired, because of a number of factors: if the circulation drops, the editor gets the blame; the editor has not only to please the public in order to keep his job, he also has to please his proprietor (much more difficult), who may view with distaste some of the circulation tricks that make his newspaper successful. Yet if the proprietor and the editor don't get on well together, the editor usually goes.

I wasn't fired. But I did lose my job because the *CDM* folded, and this – together with my self-imposed training as a freelance writer for American magazines – gave me a chance to build an entirely new life, that of a foreign correspondent. I had never filed a cable in my life, only asked others to send cables for me. It was as though I had been born again. I saw the world through different eyes and my life – except for the partings from Titina – was one long adventure.

I felt as though my vocation was to chase deadlines. From time to time I tried to engineer assignments on which Titina could join me. In Cairo, the foreign editor suggested that I should spend ten days working on an in-depth series about the problems facing the Copts in Nasser's new Egypt.

One happy Thursday I phoned Titina in Switzerland, telling her that she could safely spend at least a week in Cairo. She caught the first available plane, arriving in Cairo on the evening of the following day, a Friday. All was set for a wonderful time. On the Saturday Makarias was deported from Cyprus, and I was whisked off to Athens. Poor Titina! She must be the only tourist to have visited Egypt without seeing the pyramids.

Another new life was born when I nearly died in the car crash in 1960. For me it was the end of one life. No more hopping in and out of helicopters or chartered single-engined planes to beat the opposition. I was, as I have

related, desk-bound at the age of fifty-one and though I
soon compromised by working only nine months of the
year for the *Mail*, I was never really happy. I was used to
taking orders from editors, and cheerfully abiding by most
of their suggestions, but that had changed. Since I was
now syndication manager, I had to deal with management
men, and quite a few of them I didn't like at all – particularly those who were pompous, inclined to fat, and filled
with a sense of self-importance, though often with very
little knowledge of what was *really* required to make a
good newspaper and instead contenting themselves with
making a good profit. I was used to action, usually receiving
my orders on the telephone because time was so precious.
Now I would get a letter asking me for some useless
information that I could easily have phoned through to the
man who had dictated the memo from the vast distance of
one floor above mine.

There were many exceptions of course – Bobby Redhead, 'Duke' Hussey (before he left to become Managing
Director of *The Times*). Duke it was who overruled the
minor official in charge of dishing out office cars, and gave
me an XJ6.

'I'll call it an extra bonus for Hungary and the South
Pole,' he said. Duke was followed by one other managing
director who is still, many years later, a firm friend: 'Mick'
Shields, a human dynamo – and by that I mean not only
a dynamo, but very, very human.

Still, I was restless. The non-fiction books like *Sinister
Twilight* in particular had brought me some critical acclaim,
but only because of the hard slog of working at two jobs
(and managing Syndication *was* a hard slog, even though
I had a staff of thirty-two). I yearned for a new life – the
last but one of my many very different lives. No, I didn't
become a novelist yet, but I did become a full-time writer,
my first youthful ambition which had originated when I
wrote my first unsuccessful book at the age of seventeen
or eighteen.

The man responsible was my literary agent, George
Greenfield. He had dealt with my affairs after James Kinross had died. George is not only content to handle a
manuscript, but is the sort of man who is always imagining
the kind of fortunes that could result if only a writer
would follow his advice. (No better example of George's
persistence is the way in which he continually encouraged
David Niven to start writing. He virtually had to force out
of Niven those wonderful books which made millions.)

By now I had published nearly thirty books, many translated, and one day over lunch, as usual at the Empress,
George said, 'I've been looking at your royalty statements
and though I know you're well paid at the *Mail* [I was by
now a director of the main board] my bet is that by working
three months a year, as you are doing, you are making
more out of your books than you do in nine months at the
Daily Mail. And by starting work on books at seven in
the morning, then switching to the *Mail*, then working
Saturdays and Sundays at home – well, it doesn't make
sense.'

I had never realised that. I'm not being silly when I
honestly say that I never think about money as long as I
have enough to enjoy the best of everything (as someone
more famous than me said). We had a lovely old house in
the King's Road, a cottage with five acres in the country,
my free XJ6, and an innate hatred of night-clubs which I
always regarded in my Paris days as a place to go only in
order to get to know someone more intimately, since
dancing really is the next best thing to sex.

'You could earn twice as much if you were a full-time
writer,' George persisted.

That was what settled it. Not the money, but that phrase
from my youthful dreams, 'a full-time writer . . .'

Within a week I had arranged to take voluntary retirement. I was on the verge of sixty-five anyway, but Esmond
and I had reached a verbal understanding (at his sugges-
tion) that no compulsory retirement would ever apply to
me. It was his way of repaying my loyalty to him and

acknowledging the gruelling life I had led. 'When *you* want to take it easy – if ever,' he had said, 'come and arrange it with me.' Now that time had come. And everything went smoothly. The office not only gave me a very good pension, they even gave me my XJ6! And so on my birthday, September 9th 1974, I started yet another new life, as a full-time professional writer. The next time I applied for a new passport I was able to change my occupation from 'journalist' to 'author'.

And there this book might have ended, for I was making a comfortable living, and in the course of the seventies I wrote, with much care because I had more time, several books, most of them successful enough to pay the food bill (caviar, thank God, is very overrated).

But George is a patient, persistent fellow, and I suppose I must have been sixty-nine when he started nagging me again.

'Such a waste!' he sighed. 'When I think of the life you've led, to say nothing' – with a sly aside – 'of the exciting women you used to know,' adding hurriedly, 'before you married Titina of course.'

'Why such a waste?'

'Well, why not have a crack at a novel? Think of the life you've lived and the different characters you've met. Damn it, you wouldn't even have to invent anything.'

'A novel at the age of seventy!'

'Why not? You'd describe all the backgrounds without even looking at a street plan – think of Singapore, Cairo, the South Seas, the twelve years you lived in France. All you'd have to do would be to invent a few situations and put them into places you know, fill them with people you've known in the past – and you could even work in real events.'

'Not on.' I signalled to Negri to bring the bill. 'I like doing my non-fiction books, and I know I can earn a big enough advance to live on before I've written a single word.'

For though I would never make a fortune out of my

non-fiction books, I certainly enjoyed life; and the research
of my helpers was so meticulous that the facts were rarely
in dispute.

All the same, as I reached King's Road and the quiet of
my study, with its old-fashioned Victorian mahogany desk
and its book-lined walls, I did admit to a slight pang for
the last unfulfilled dream of youth. I had had – was still
enjoying – a life that excited the envy of all my friends.
Yet, ironically, I had failed in one dream of my youth: to
become a novelist. All those years since I was a youngster
I had been so busy living different lives – and making
enough money to enjoy them – that I had in a sense been
trapped. As I argued to myself, you can't go on changing
lives, specially when you've reached the magic – if dismal
– milestone of three score years and ten.

But just supposing . . . No, it was ridiculous! Was it?
No. Well, maybe. Had it been ridiculous when, as an
editor, I had at the ripe old age of forty-three become a
globe-trotting foreign correspondent? Had it been ridiculous, at the even riper age of sixty-five, to leave the security
of a job which I could keep for life, with a newspaper for
which I had worked for thirty-four years, in order to
become a full-time writer, whose income would depend
on continuing good health as much as on ability? If I had
to spend a few weeks or months in hospital through no
fault of my own my income would cease – whereas after
my car crash the *Mail* had continued to pay my salary for
nearly a year without a second thought. So to embark –
purely on a selfish gamble – on an entirely new life (with,
be it said, the need for new thought processes) would be
mad unless I had a million in the bank – and that I never
would have.

Over our pre-dinner drinks I said to Titina, 'George
wants me to write a novel. He said, "Let's go for the
jackpot".' I laughed. 'Imagine at my age!'

'Wouldn't it be fantastic if you *did* win the jackpot,' she
said.

'Like winning the pools?'

'More satisfying – because of the challenge.'

'I know.' I poured out a second scotch with water but no ice. 'But even if I *did* write a novel, even if I *did* get it published, I'd probably only get a few thousand pounds for it and it would sink without trace – whereas with non-fiction I earn a good living.'

'Even if you didn't make a fortune, you would have a novel on your shelves – and that's what you wanted when you were young,' said Titina. 'It would be an achievement – and to you, that's as important as the money.'

That was true. I had just finished correcting the proofs of my latest book called *The Fall of Shanghai* and after a week of private agonising, I rang up George.

'I'll have a go at it!' I said.

'Great!' he cried, and added some curious advice. 'But if you really mean it, don't tell anyone about it till we've discussed the project. I'll explain why over lunch. By the way, any ideas?'

I had thought that out – if I did write a novel, it had to be based on truth.

'Sure,' I said. 'I'd like to write a big book about Singapore – spanning two or three generations from the turn of the century, through the war, and ending with independence.'

'Wonderful.' Start to draft an outline and we'll talk next week.'

I did draft the outline of *Tanamera*, the book that was to change my life, but it was thanks to George that it became an international bestseller, eventually translated into fifteen languages. For, though I had to do the writing, he laid his plans carefully, and since this book was never 'hyped' (the term used for promoting books that are not worth promoting) I can explain George's tactics without embarrassment on my part.

'The outline of forty pages is fine,' he said, 'but don't let one single British publisher know what you're doing.'

While I listened, slightly mystified, he explained that if I offered the synopsis together with say, five or six chapters,

to a British publisher, I would be regarded as just another
foreign correspondent trying to break into the fiction market.

'Well, isn't that true?'

'Maybe. But in America, where the publishing houses
don't really know of your adventures as a foreign correspondent – or even that you once lived in Singapore – it
will be regarded as a first novel about a country that few
novelists have written about.'

Well, that is just what happened. Macmillan in America
bought the book on the basis of the outline and five
chapters, and as soon as the news appeared in *Publishers
Weekly* it was bought in England by Hodder & Stoughton.

The writing of the book was, for me, pure joy, perhaps
because Singapore was the first tropical island I had ever
lived on. I had also done my homework by writing *Sinister
Twilight*, a non-fiction book dealing with events leading to
the Japanese victory in Singapore. And then I remembered
some of the advice that Willie Maugham had given me
when we discussed writing novels years previously during
one of my weekends at St Jean Cap Ferrat.

We were sitting near the pool in the magnificent grounds
at the Villa Mauresque, in the 'White Garden', a section
of his property where every bloom was white – one of his
favourite spots.

'Never invent more than you have to,' he said, 'especially, my dear boy, with the locality of scenes.' Adding
with his usual touch of asperity, 'Most would-be novelists
who fail to achieve success do so because they think that
their own lives are too drab to write about. So they invent
scenes in glamorous places which they know nothing
about.'

It was advice that I carried out to the letter. In *Tanamera
no* scenes were invented. The great house called Tanamera
was a carbon copy of the house of a rich director of the
Malaya Tribune. The 'Cadet House' where Julie and John
Dexter first lived together was my own flat when I lived in
Singapore. It's still there, and I saw it in 1984, the last time

I was in Singapore. The office of Dexter & Co was also a carbon copy of the *Tribune* offices where I worked. Grandpa Jack was based on my grandfather. Papa Jack was in part a copy of my own father. The Chinese millionaire was also based on a real character. And as for Julie, she was based on a real person with whom, in the distant past, I had had a love affair.

In the next novels I used the same technique. In *A Farewell to France* the family flat was my own flat, even down to the address. The *Paris Weekly* was the *CDM*, even down to the address. The château at Douzy is based on a real château; the small cottage of the 'Misses B & B' was my own country cottage. Sonia was based on a real person with whom I also fell in love – though at a different time!

One of the most intriguing facets of *France* is the description of the tunnel at Rilly where the Germans stored dangerous weapons, including components for V2 rockets. It is all based on truth. For weeks during the war the inhabitants of Rilly couldn't understand why the RAF should bomb this small village so mercilessly, night after night, as they did. Only after the War did I by chance learn that the RAF *knew* that it was imperative to block the tunnel. In *France* I blocked it off in a more dramatic fashion.

As for the terrible stream of refugees following the fall of Paris, I followed every inch of that route to Bordeaux, taking nearly three months to re-live the incidents. And of course, I did know most of the characters – Madame de Portes, Reynaud (whom I met again by chance on a cruise after the War), and I visited Laval in Fresnes jail on the day before he was shot. I remember he complained bitterly about a boil on the back of his neck which he insisted needed medical attention! I also spent day after day at the trial of Pétain. So I knew my background.

I did the same with *A Woman of Cairo*. I was staying at Shepheards, researching a piece for the *Saturday Evening Post*, when the hotel was burned down in 1952.

I knew Nasser and Sadat *before* they took power because for years I had worshipped at the feet of one of Fleet Street's greatest foreign correspondents, the late Ward Price, who once gave me this advice: 'If you're interested in a country that looks unstable, pick out a dozen or so men contending for future power and get to know them well in advance.' That was why Ward Price was able to obtain exclusive interviews with both Hitler and Mussolini; they were 'friends' of his because he had cultivated them in good time. In the same way I had met Nasser and Sadat and even arranged interviews at the Abdin Palace where I was introduced to Farouk, and attended a great dinner from which I pinched the exotic menu card. Later of course, I depicted Serena in this setting, the night she went to her first ball which I was able to describe in such detail.

The crash scene in the desert on the way to Alexandria is modelled on the crash I was involved in when four people, in the other car, were killed; when I had a touch of heart trouble, I actually copied out the doctors' reports on my condition and used them as the reason why Greg couldn't join the army.

The setting of my latest book (as yet untitled) is the South Seas – shades of Tom Neale, Aggy Grey, and her famous hotel in Apia, where I once spent some time; shades, too, of the three months spent writing in Moorea.

Finally, and just in case some aspiring novelist would like to know the mechanics of writing a novel, this is the way I work.

When I have an idea based on a locale I know, I draft a short synopsis (not necessarily definitive) and George Greenfield reads it and decides whether to carry on. If he does, I start work.

I get up at seven every morning, seven days a week, start work at eight, write one thousand words, usually by 12.30, which is the moment I sip my first pink gin (Plymouth, please). I write in longhand. I find it less inhibiting – easier to change words than having to roll back a typed page and not finding room for insertions. When I am writing I always follow the invaluable advice Willie Maugham gave me:

'Write everything in exercise books,' he suggested, 'using the right-hand pages only. Then you can use the left-hand pages for inserting material later.' When the first draft with its insertions has been typed, the pages (he explained) should be put into a loose-leaf binder so that this procedure could be repeated as many times as necessary on the typed pages. Another of his suggestions was to number the pages of each chapter separately in case one wished to insert some pages in a chapter in the middle of a book.

One piece of Maugham's advice I have never been able to follow: 'The trouble with you journalists,' he said in his reedy voice, 'is that often you don't know how you're going to finish a paragraph when you start to write it. Why don't you think things out?'

Easier said than written, after years of rushing cables to beat deadlines.

And there's one last piece of advice which Willie gave me. 'If you ever get stuck, or over-enthusiastic about a scene which you know you will want to write later, don't wait. Even if it's several chapters ahead of the narrative you are writing, get it out of your system.'

I do this regularly; I penned the description of the fire in Cairo six months before I reached that point in the narrative because a desire to get the story on paper niggled me to such an extent that it interfered with the section I was supposed to be writing at the time. Once I had got the fire out of the way, I had no problem with the earlier section.

One final piece of advice given to me by Noël Coward: 'Never finish the day's work at the end of a scene if you can help it,' he told me. 'If you are halfway through a dramatic episode, it is much easier to start work the next morning, my dear boy.'

And that's all there is to it really. Except that last year, Titina and I, the kids and their friends, spent a glamorous six weeks in a large Tuscan farmhouse which we rented from a friend. It slept fourteen, had a huge pool, and was perched on top of a hill in a tiny village near Lucca, with the improbable name of Massaciuccoli.

A week or so before we were due to leave London on our holiday, I discovered that my passport had expired. How time flies! It seemed so recently that my occupation had changed from 'journalist' to 'author'.

Here I was once again at London's Petty France. It seemed a golden opportunity to change my life officially for the very last time. So, with barely a tear of regret, I bade farewell to the author who had served me so well, and introduced myself to the latest Noel Barber: Occupation, Novelist.

NOEL BARBER

A FAREWELL TO FRANCE

Sonia Riccardi, impetuous and sensual, was a woman
no man could resist. And Larry Astell, heir to a champagne fortune, knew their passion was the most important part of his life. Until war placed in jeopardy all they
held dear – love, family, country.

From the Left Bank of the 1930s to Nazi-occupied Paris,
A FAREWELL TO FRANCE is an epic novel of star-
crossed lovers torn apart by duty to a cause and de-
votion to others.

POSTA LITTLE HAPPINESS

Post·A·Book

A Royal Mail service in association with the Book Marketing Council & The Booksellers Association.
Post-A-Book is a Post Office trademark.

NOEL BARBER

TANAMERA

The spellbinding story of two lovers and two great dynasties; one British, the other Chinese, the society that separated them and the passion that bound them.

TANAMERA sweeps from the steamy, British-ruled Malaya of the 1930s through the bloody days of the Japanese occupation, to the tumultuous birth of a nation. At its centre is John Dexter, heir to a fabulous financial empire, and Julie Soong, daughter of Singapore's richest and most powerful Chinese family. Their love was as forbidden as it was inevitable and the price they had to pay for it was beyond their wildest dreams . . .

HODDER AND STOUGHTON PAPERBACKS

NOEL BARBER

A WOMAN OF CAIRO

A grand and passionate drama set in Egypt in the tumultuous decades culminating in World War II.

In the turbulent years when Egypt progresses from a corrupt monarchy to a fledgling democracy, Mark Holt and Serena Sirry grow up to discover a love for each other so strong that time, war, and even the wrath of kings cannot destroy it.

As the storms of war threaten this ancient and exotic land, the lovers – each trapped in loveless marriages – are forced to part. Evan as fate seems intent upon separating them, an unbreakable bond carries them through to the powerful climax of this irresistible saga: Mark's defence of Serena in an Egyptian court – against a change of murder.

'A story as majestic and fertile as its setting ... always entertaining'

Publishers Weekly

HODDER AND STOUGHTON PAPERBACKS

NOEL BARBER

THE OTHER SIDE OF PARADISE

A sweeping, exotic novel set on an island paradise between the wars.

London 1937. Following a street fight with a fascist Blackshirt, young pioneering doctor Kit Masters is forced to flee England and make a new start in life.

Arriving on the South Sea island of Koraloona, he soon becomes enchanted by the place and its people. With the eccentric Doc Reid, he dreams of building a hospital. With Aleena, beautiful daughter of the island's princess, he dreams of a life together.

But as Kit and Aleena fall passionately in love the coming of war threatens to change their island paradise forever.

'With amiable ease, Barber evokes the last minutes of the British Empire'

The Mail on Sunday

HODDER AND STOUGHTON PAPERBACKS

NOEL BARBER

THE WEEPING AND THE LAUGHTER

Some families are fated to live out their lives among the dramas and turmoil of great events.

Such are the Korolevs.

In 1919, as the Russian revolution threatens to engulf them, Prince Dimitri and his family flee for their lives. The Princess is killed, the twins, Nicki and Rudi, separated.

Escaping to Switzerland and then to France, joined by Aunt Olga and his cousin Natasha, Nicki grows up amongst all the swirling artistic excitement of Paris in the Twenties: the dancers, the painters, the high society and the *demi monde*. All is adventure and discovery and Nicki falls passionately in love.

But the violent upheavals of the Second World War are looming. In the chaos and uncertainty, Nicki gets word that his long lost brother Rudi may still be alive. At the same time, his love affair with Natasha seems doomed.

As the rising tides of war surge and crash about them, as people and relationships are forced apart and flung together, a storm tossed climax of danger and violent emotion is bearing down on them all.

'Full of dramatic events and passionate people growing up in troubled war-torn times. Compelling'
Woman's World

HODDER AND STOUGHTON PAPERBACKS

MAEVE BINCHY

LIGHT A PENNY CANDLE

'The most enchanting book I have read since GONE
WITH THE WIND'
Sunday Telegraph

Compassionate and delightful, this is the magnificent
story of twenty turbulent years in the lives of two
women. One is English, the other is Irish. Their friendship is sealed when they are children: it is warm, devoted, unshakeable and, against all odds, it survives.
Their names are Aisling and Elizabeth . . .

'Thank heavens – a thoroughly enjoyable and readable
book'
The Times

'Brilliant: a remarkable, panoramic and vastly entertaining novel'
Molly Keane, Irish Press

'A marvellous first novel which combines those rare
talents of storytelling and memorable writing'
Jeffrey Archer

HODDER AND STOUGHTON PAPERBACKS

MAEVE BINCHY

ECHOES

A compelling story of love, friendship, ambition and duty.

Ireland in the Fifties. Three children from very different backgrounds are growing up in the tiny seaside town of Castlebay. Clare dreams of escape through education and David of a dazzling future as a specialist doctor. Gerry just wants fame and success. Over the next decade their lives are destined to meet in a quite unforeseen way, but never will they escape the echoes of their past.

'Ms Binchy has the true story-teller's knack'

Observer

'It left me stunned'

Daily Express

HODDER AND STOUGHTON PAPERBACKS

MAEVE BINCHY

VICTORIA LINE, CENTRAL LINE

From Seven Sisters to Stockwell, from Shepherd's Bush to Chancery Lane, everyday life is never as dull as it might seem.

At Oxford Street two former rivals plot a murder; at Bond Street a shoplifter avoids the sales assistant's eye; at Tottenham Hale Amy worries about her domineering sister-in-law . . .

With characteristic humour and originality, Maeve Binchy has exposed an enthralling, wonderfully realistic cross-section of London life.

'Reading these tales is like listening to someone talking: someone you very much want to hear'
Sunday Telegraph

'Rare delights from an inveterate storyteller'
New Society

HODDER AND STOUGHTON PAPERBACKS

MAEVE BINCHY

FIREFLY SUMMER

Everything was changing. The big man from the States was here, with a dream in his heart and money in his pocket. With plans for Mountfern.

Sleepy little Mountfern, where people go quietly about their business – while taking a deep interest in everyone else's business. Where the big house, Fernscourt, burned down in the Troubles, has for years been no more than an ivy-clad playground for the village children. Patrick O'Neill's arrival will change all this: Fernscourt will be turned into a sophisticated hotel catering to Americans; and by summer's end new friendships, passions and tragedy will have destroyed the lulling surface calm of Mountfern life.

'An enchanting story of tangled emotions and changing times'

Over 21

'How wise and funny Maeve Binchy is'

The Irish Times

HODDER AND STOUGHTON PAPERBACKS

ALSO AVAILABLE FROM
HODDER AND STOUGHTON PAPERBACKS